A Student's Guide to Harmony and Counterpoint

for AS and A2 Music

by

Hugh Benham

Edited by Paul Terry

Rhinegold Publishing Ltd
241 Shaftesbury Avenue
London WC2H 8TF

Rhinegold Music Study Guides
(series editor: Paul Terry)

A Student's Guide to GCSE Music (separate volumes for the AQA, Edexcel and OCR specifications)
A Student's Guide to GCSE Music for the WJEC Specification (separate English and Welsh language versions)

A Student's Guide to AS Music (separate volumes for the AQA, Edexcel and OCR specifications)
A Student's Guide to A2 Music (separate volumes for the AQA, Edexcel and OCR specifications)
A Student's Guide to AS/A2 Music Technology for the Edexcel AS and A2 Specification

GCSE Listening Tests, Books 1 and 2 (separate volumes for the AQA, Edexcel and OCR specifications)
AS/A2 Listening Tests (separate volumes for AQA Music and for Edexcel Music Technology)
AS Listening Tests (in separate volumes: Books 1 and 2 for Edexcel, and Book 1 for OCR)
A2 Listening Tests (in separate volumes: Books 1 and 2 for Edexcel, and Book 1 for OCR)

A Student's Guide to Composing (Book 1 for GCSE and Book 2 for A-level Music)
A Student's Guide to Harmony and Counterpoint (for AS and A2 Music)

Other Rhinegold Study Guides

Students' Guides to AS and A2 Drama and Theatre Studies for the AQA and Edexcel Specifications
Students' Guides to AS and A2 Performance Studies for the OCR Specification
Students' Guides to AS and A2 Religious Studies for the AQA, Edexcel and OCR Specifications

Rhinegold Publishing also publishes Classical Music, Classroom Music, Early Music Today, Music Teacher,
Opera Now, Piano, Teaching Drama, The Singer, British and International Music Yearbook, British Performing
Arts Yearbook, Rhinegold Guide to Music Education, Rhinegold Dictionary of Music in Sound.

First published 2006 in Great Britain by
Rhinegold Publishing Limited
241 Shaftesbury Avenue
London WC2H 8TF
Telephone: 020 7333 1720
Fax: 020 7333 1765
www.rhinegold.co.uk

© Rhinegold Publishing Limited 2006
Reprinted 2006, 2007

If you are preparing for an exam in music you should always carefully check
the current requirements of the examination, since these may change from one year to the next.

A Student's Guide to Harmony and Counterpoint
British Library Cataloguing in Publication Data.
A catalogue record for this book is available from the British Library.

ISBN 978-1-904226-31-4

Printed in Great Britain by WPG Group Ltd

Contents

About the author

Hugh Benham has been involved in the examining of A-level and GCE Music since 1981. For 20 years he was head of the music department in a large sixth-form college, and has considerable experience in adult education and in-service training. He is also a church organist. Dr Benham contributed to *The New Grove Dictionary of Music and Musicians* (2001) and is the author of two books on English church music, one of which, *John Taverner: his Life and Music* was published by Ashgate in 2003. He has contributed to *Music Teacher* and *Classroom Music* magazines, has written articles on early music, and was the editor of Taverner's complete works for *Early English Church Music* (published by Stainer and Bell for The British Academy).

Author's acknowledgements

I would particularly like to thank David Bowman for his extensive preparatory work on this book, and Paul Terry for his many editorial suggestions. The experience of both as former Chief Examiners in Music for Edexcel has been especially valuable. I should also like to thank my colleague, Bruce Cole, for his advice and assistance. Nevertheless, if any errors have been made it is only right to state that these are the responsibility of the author. Finally, I would like to thank Dr Lucien Jenkins and Jonathan Wikeley of Rhinegold Publishing for their help and encouragement in the preparation of this Study Guide.

Introduction

Who this Guide is written for

This book is designed for *you*, if you are studying, or about to study, harmony and counterpoint ('compositional techniques') as part of an AS or A2 qualification.

✦ If you are preparing for an Edexcel exam, you will find guidance on the four most popular topics – chorale harmonisation, baroque counterpoint, middle eights in 32-bar pop songs, and serialism

✦ If you are preparing for an OCR or WJEC exam, or for the techniques option in CCEA AS Music, you should find the chapters on chorales and baroque two-part counterpoint useful.

Remember that if you are studying for an examination, you and your teacher should carefully check the current exam requirements, since these may change from one year to the next. Each awarding body makes exam specifications available on its website, and each can provide past papers for you to practise.

This book should be useful also for revision and consolidation if you are studying harmony and counterpoint at a music college or reading music at a university.

What's in the Guide?

Part I provides material that will enable you to approach with confidence the specific techniques to be studied in Part II. It begins with a chapter on keys and intervals – even if you already know most or all of this information, it will still be useful for revision and for reference. In Chapter 2 you will learn about the most widely-used kinds of chords – triads and 7th chords. Chapter 3 shows how chords are used one after another to form 'progressions'. Chapter 4 deals with the general principles of part-writing or voice-leading, and with notes that are not part of a chord. Chapter 5 looks at counterpoint, in which each part enjoys much more melodic and rhythmic independence than in the mostly chordal writing seen in the earlier chapters.

Part II deals in detail with four specific types of techniques test set in AS and A2 exams. Here you need only study the chapters about the options you are taking.

A reference section at the end of the book includes advice on using score-writing software for answers, and some help on writing for different types of instrument.

Activities

All the chapters include activities to help you learn and remember what you have read. These are not just exercises to write out. They are there to help you think in terms of real sounds. So it is important to sing, hum, whistle or play everything. Don't worry about the sound you make so long as the pitches are correct. Use whatever assistance you can muster – ask a friend or teacher to play your work, notate it on screen and play it back through the speakers on your computer, play four-part harmony as a piano duet – the options are endless.

Consult if in doubt!

Many technical terms will be explained as we go along, but if anything is not clear, do not gloss over it – ask your teacher for help.

What you need to know before starting Chapter 1

It is really important that you are confident about reading and writing:

✦ the notes of the treble stave
✦ time values for notes and rests (including dotted and tied notes)
✦ time signatures
✦ dynamic markings
✦ simple speed indications.

If you need to learn or revise any of these topics, please consult appropriate theory books (for example those published by the Associated Board of the Royal Schools of Music and other bodies offering graded examinations).

The bass stave You will need also to know the names of notes on the bass stave for every type of exercise (except perhaps serialism at AS). If you are uncertain of the notes of the bass stave, or would like to brush up your knowledge, please read the following.

The bass stave can be thought of as a downward extension of the treble, as you can see from the music example below. The bass clef (𝄢) derives from the letter 'F' and wraps itself around the line representing F below middle C. The example shows that by using leger lines, some notes can be written on either the treble or bass stave.

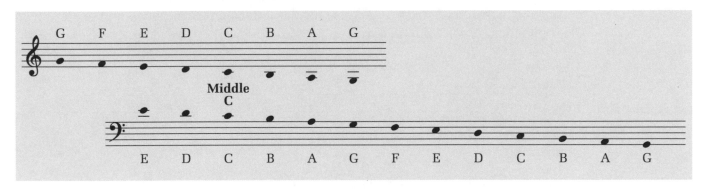

You must be able to read music on the bass stave with ease, and so you may need a lot of practice. Here are three tasks which should help. If necessary, do (c) over and over again, with plenty of different melodies.

(a) Write letter names under each note of the following tune:

Sousa: *The Liberty Bell*

(b) Write a melody you know well on a treble stave, and then rewrite it an octave or two lower on a bass stave.

(c) Find more treble-stave melodies (for example, in this book) and rewrite them an octave or two lower on a bass stave.

1   Keys and intervals

1.1   The concept of key

Most music is in a **key**, with one particular note more important than all the others. This main note is called the **tonic** or the **keynote** (or simply note 1) and it usually occurs frequently. It is also normally heard at the end of a piece, to provide a sense of completion, a feeling of arriving home.

Think, if you like, of the tonic as the sun and the other notes as the planets, some of which are more distant than others, but all of which are bound to the sun by the force of gravity.

1.2   Scales

Each key is based on a particular set of notes known as a **scale**. For instance, the key of C major is based on the scale of C major.

This kind of scale has eight notes. Numbers 1 and 8 are an octave apart and share the same letter name. Numbers 2–7 use all the letter names in between, once each, in alphabetical order, with no gaps.

The scale shown above is an **ascending** scale of C. The notes C B A G F E D C form a **descending** scale of C, falling from one C to the C an octave lower.

Why is C G E A D B F C not a scale, even though it uses exactly the same notes as the example above? Because the notes are not in alphabetical order – each one doesn't move in **stepwise** fashion to the next note in the scale. Instead there are gaps, which we call **leaps**.

1.3   Major and minor scales and keys

Two types of scales are particularly important – **major** and **minor**. Example 1.2 shows a major scale. As you would expect:

✦ major scales belong to major keys
✦ minor scales belong to minor keys.

1.4   Major scales and major keys

How can you tell that the scale shown in Example 1.2 is a major scale? First and foremost, because it *sounds* like one! The reason for the major sound is the precise pattern of notes used. For example, the E must be E(♮) not E♭, the A must be A(♮) not A♭, and so on. Play C D E♭ F G A♭ B C, and you won't hear a major scale.

Intervals will be discussed more fully later in this chapter.

The notes in Example 1.2 form a scale of C major because of the precise distances (or **intervals**) between notes. If you replaced E with E♭ you would create a narrower gap between notes 2 and 3 of the scale, and a wider gap between notes 3 and 4. In fact, you would have the wrong interval pattern for a major scale.

Every major scale has the same pattern of intervals. This is why a D-major scale, for example, sounds similar to a C-major scale, except that it is a little higher. The pattern of a C-major scale is shown again in Example 1.4.1. The letter **S** indicates a gap of a **semitone** (the smallest interval normally used in western music) and the letter **T** indicates a gap of a **tone** (an interval which is equivalent to two semitones).

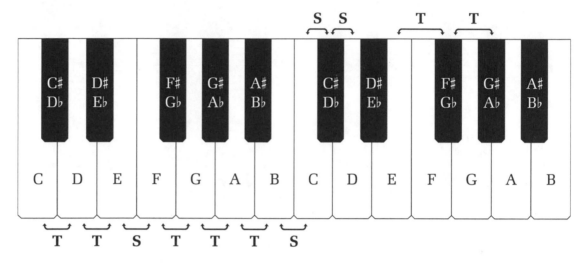

Ex. 1.4.1

T   T   S   T   T   T   S

A good way to understand tones and semitones is to look at the layout of a keyboard:

* When you move from any note (white or black) to the *very next* one on the right or left (white or black) you are moving by a semitone. The gaps between C and C♯, C♯ and D, E and F, and B and C are all semitones.

* When you move from any note (white or black) to the *next but one* on the right or left (white or black) you are moving by a tone. The gaps between C and D, D and E, E and F♯, and F♯ and G♯ are all tones.

The **T T S T T T S** pattern shown in Example 1.4.1 is the essence of all major scales. Whatever note you start on, provided you keep to the **T T S T T T S** pattern, you will hear a major scale.

Here is a complete scale of D major, with each interval marked **T** or **S**:

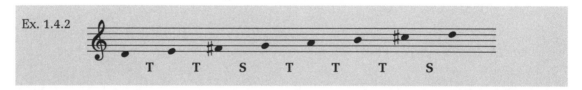

Ex. 1.4.2

T   T   S   T   T   T   S

Activity 1.4.1

Work out the notes belonging to each of the following major scales:

(i)   F major
(ii) B♭ major
(iii) E major.

Use music notation and/or write the letter names of notes. Show where the tones (**T**) and semitones (**S**) come in each scale.

See page 174 for other major scales.

Example 1.4.3 *below* shows the nine most widely-used major scales. You should aim to become familiar with all of them as soon as possible. Each scale is printed twice:

✦ In the first column the scale is shown with a sharp or flat sign placed in front of each note that needs one (in other words, **accidentals** are used).

✦ In the second column a **key signature** is provided – that is, one, two, three or four sharps or flats appear just after the treble clef to show which sharps or flats are needed. This is a useful labour-saving device, since it saves using accidentals, but note carefully the order in which the sharps or flats are written.

The third column shows you how key signatures are written in the bass clef.

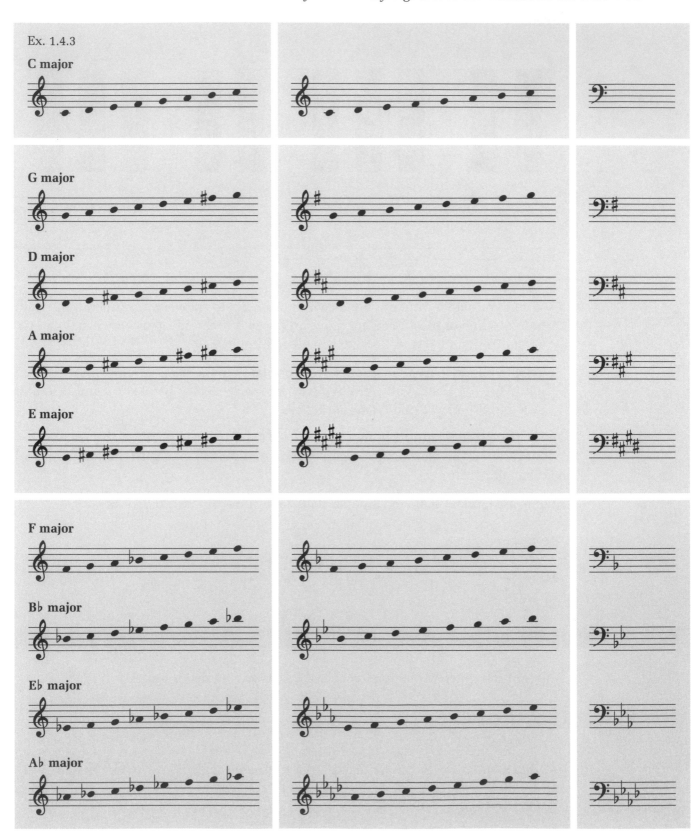

Ex. 1.4.3
C major
G major
D major
A major
E major
F major
B♭ major
E♭ major
A♭ major

It may help you remember the relationship between major scales and their key signatures if you note that:

✦ In sharp keys, the last sharp on the right of the key signature is always note 7

✦ In flat keys, the last flat on the right of the key signature is always note 4.

There are three important conventions concerning key signatures:

✦ The symbols in a key signature apply to all notes with the same letter name, whatever the octave in which they occur. For instance, in the key of G major, the F♯ in the key signature means that *every* F is actually F♯, whatever the octave in which it occurs.

✦ The sharps or flats in a key signature are always shown in the order you see them in Example 1.4.3 *opposite*.

✦ A key signature always comes *before* a time signature, not after it.

Activity 1.4.2

Write one octave of each of the following major scales in the bass clef. Do not use key signatures but add all necessary sharp or flat signs. Show where the tones (**T**) and semitones (**S**) come.

(i) F major   (ii) G major   (iii) D major   (iv) A major   (v) A♭ major

If this is all rather new to you, study the bass-clef key signatures in Example 1.4.3 to help you see which sharp or flat signs will be needed, but do take the time to learn how to work out each scale for yourself.

1.5 Degree numbers and names

Earlier the numbers 1–8 were used to refer to the various notes of a scale. But because people often use **degree names** (words such as tonic and supertonic) instead, you will need to get to know these as well:

Numbers	Degree names	Example Scale of D major	Tonic sol-fa
1	Tonic	D	doh
2	Supertonic	E	ray
3	Mediant	F♯	me
4	Subdominant	G	fa
5	Dominant	A	soh
6	Submediant	B	lah
7	Leading note	C♯	te
8 (=1)	Tonic	D	doh

The last column in this table shows the tonic sol-fa names (doh, ray, me etc.) of the notes in a major scale. They can be helpful when you have to sing, play or imagine a melody, but if you are not familiar with these names you do not need to learn them.

Note that from now on examples will not always be based on C major. Keys such as D major are used just as widely and are not really any more difficult.

(a) Write one octave *ascending* of each of the following scales:

On a treble stave: E major, B♭ major, A♭ major.
On a bass stave: E major, E♭ major.

Write each scale (i) with accidentals, and (ii) with a key signature. Label the tones and semitones (**T** or **S**) and write the number of each note (1–8).

If this is new to you, begin by copying from Example 1.4.3 if you wish. But do take the time to learn how to work out each scale for yourself.

(b) Write, using accidentals (*not* key signatures), one octave *descending* of each of the following scales:

On a treble stave: F major, E♭ major.
On a bass stave: D major, A♭ major.

(c) Give the degree names and numbers, plus the letter names, for each degree of the G-major scale. Begin as follows: Tonic = 1 = G.

(d) A well-known melody begins: 8 8 7 6 6 5 5 4 3 3 4 5 1 2 4 3 2 1. Write the pitches in C major on a treble stave. If you know the melody, try to notate the rhythm as well.

(e) In what key is the melody below? Label each note with its degree number (1–8). The final note is marked for you: 2(♯). Which degree of the scale never appears in this excerpt?

Joplin: *The Easy Winners*

2(♯)

1.6 Minor scales and minor keys

Each major key has a related minor key, called the **relative minor**, which has the same key signature. The notes of a relative minor scale can be found by starting three semitone steps below the tonic of the major scale. For example, the relative minor of C major is A minor.

Minor scales rise in steps, using every letter name once, just like major scales, and they follow any sharps or flats given in the key signature. However, note 7 of a minor scale (and sometimes also note 6) is frequently raised a semitone by means of an accidental.

Ex. 1.6.1

Raising a note by a semitone often means sharpening it, as shown on the first stave of Example 1.6.1. But if the note concerned is a flat, as is the case with the B♭ on the second stave of the example, then you need a natural sign (♮) to raise it.

If you need the normal version of one of these altered notes later in the same bar, you will have to cancel the effect of the accidental. For instance, you would need to write G♮ to cancel the effect of G♯, or B♭ to cancel the effect of B♮.

In Example 1.6.2 *opposite*, (a) – (c) show the three forms that a scale of A minor can take, due to the different permutations of raising notes 6 and 7. The scale of A major is shown in (d) for comparison.

Ex. 1.6.2

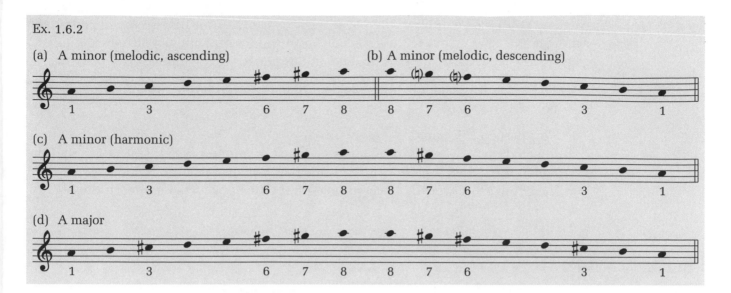

(a) A minor (melodic, ascending)

(b) A minor (melodic, descending)

(c) A minor (harmonic)

(d) A major

In Example 1.6.2 (a), notes 6 and 7 of the A-minor scale are both raised by a semitone. This form of the scale is usually found in ascending melodic passages and is known as the **ascending melodic minor**. It is very similar to A major, shown in (d), except that note 3 is a semitone lower.

In Example 1.6.2 (b) notes 6 and 7 are in their unaltered state (the natural signs are only needed if F♯ and/or G♯ appeared earlier in the same bar). Use of the unraised versions of 6 and 7 is typical of descending melodic passages, and this form of the scale is known as the **descending melodic minor**. This scale is often known as the 'natural minor' (or aeolian mode) in pop music and jazz, where it may be used in both ascending and descending melodies.

In Example 1.6.2 (c) only note 7 is raised, and so requires an accidental. The unraised sixth degree and raised seventh degree are separated by three semitones. This can sound awkward, and rarely appears in melodies. However, the type of minor scale shown in Example 1.6.2 (c) is ideal when you want to create chords. It is called the **harmonic minor** scale and is the same in both ascending and descending forms.

Activity 1.6.1

(a) Look at these four scales and label each one as either D ascending melodic minor, D descending melodic minor, D harmonic minor or D major. Remember that you need to look at notes 6 and 7 to differentiate between the various forms of minor scales, and at note 3 to distinguish between a major scale and a minor scale.

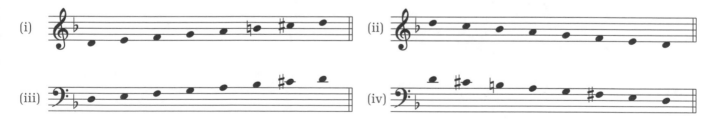

(i) (ii) (iii) (iv)

(b) What is the relative minor of D major? Remember, that to find the relative minor you count down three semitone steps from the tonic of the major scale. Now write out one octave of the harmonic minor scale of that minor key, on a treble stave.

(c) On a bass stave, write out the complete melodic minor scale, ascending and descending, of E minor.

See page 174 for other minor scales.

Example 1.6.3 *below* shows the harmonic minor scales for nine of the most widely-used minor keys – first with accidentals only, and then with key signature plus any necessary accidentals. To find the melodic minor scale, remember that:

✦ The ascending melodic minor scale differs from the harmonic in having a raised note 6.

✦ The descending melodic minor differs from the harmonic minor in having a lowered note 7. It only needs an accidental when one is necessary to cancel the effect of a raised 7 earlier in the same bar. For instance, in D minor you would have to write C♮ for the lowered seventh if C♯ had occurred earlier in the bar.

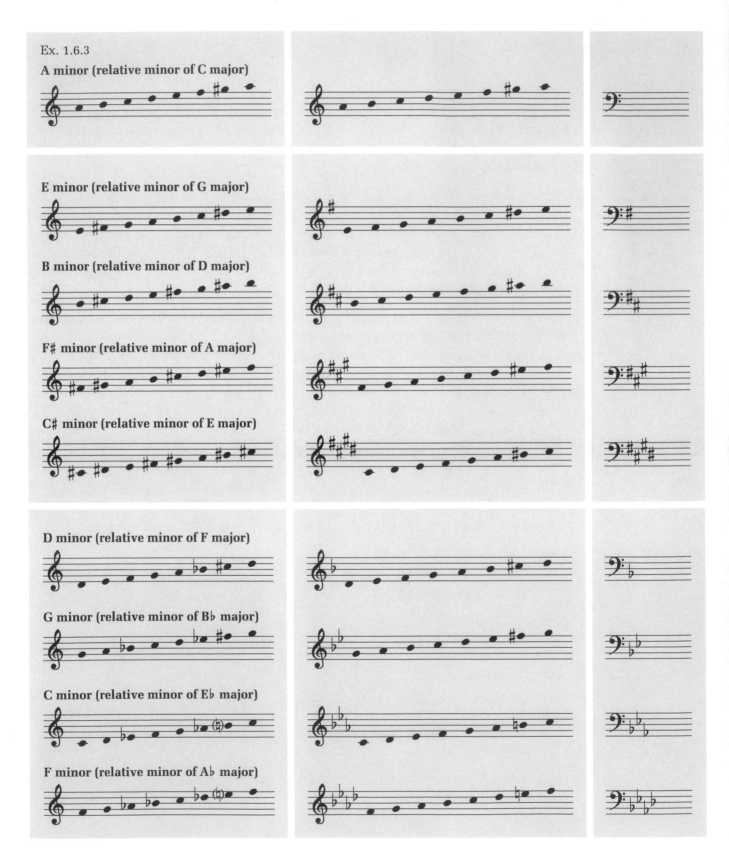

Ex. 1.6.3

A minor (relative minor of C major)

E minor (relative minor of G major)

B minor (relative minor of D major)

F♯ minor (relative minor of A major)

C♯ minor (relative minor of E major)

D minor (relative minor of F major)

G minor (relative minor of B♭ major)

C minor (relative minor of E♭ major)

F minor (relative minor of A♭ major)

(a) Write all three forms (ascending melodic, descending melodic and harmonic) of the following scales on a bass stave:

D minor, E minor, B minor, G minor, C minor, F♯ minor, F minor, C♯ minor.

Write each scale (i) with accidentals, and (ii) with a key signature. Label each note with its correct scale number (1–8).

(b) Write, using accidentals, one octave of each of the following ascending melodic minor scales on a treble stave:

D minor, B minor, G minor.

Label each note with its correct scale number of each note (1–8).

(c) Write a table showing the degree names and numbers, plus the letter names, for each note in the following scales:

G harmonic minor, F melodic minor (ascending), E melodic minor (descending).

Begin your first table as follows: Tonic = 1 = G.

(d) In what key are the two phrases below? (Notice that the second one is in the bass clef). Label each note of the melody below with its degree number (1–8).

Iona community: *Jubilate, everybody*

Iona community: *Jubilate, everybody*

1.7 Two final points about minor keys

So far we have considered each minor key in relation to its relative major, since both have the same key signature, although they have different key notes.

The tonic minor

But what about major and minor scales that start on the same tonic, such as C major and C minor? They are referred to as tonic major and tonic minor respectively, and although they have different key signatures, they relate to each other like this:

✦ Note 3 (the mediant) is a semitone lower in the tonic minor key. It makes the interval of a *minor* 3rd above note 1, not a major 3rd and is the main thing that differentiates minor and major scales which start on the same key note.

✦ Notes 1, 2, 4 and 5 are always the same in tonic major and tonic minor scales.

✦ Notes 6 and 7 may be the same in the tonic major and tonic minor scales, but more often note 6 (and sometimes note 7) is a semitone lower in the minor.

From all of this, we can see that the main difference between tonic major and tonic minor is that note 3 is a semitone lower in the latter.

Naming minor keys

Although there are different forms of minor scale, we do not say that a piece is in, for example, 'C harmonic minor'. We just say that it is in C minor, because composers don't generally restrict themselves to a single form of the scale.

1.8 Melodic and harmonic intervals

An interval is the distance between two pitches. If the two notes sound one after the other, they form a **melodic interval**. If they sound at the same time, they form an **harmonic interval**. Intervals are the building blocks of melody and harmony, and you must understand them in terms of both sound and notation.

Harmonic intervals are discussed later, in section **1.13**.

1.9 Counting intervals by letter names

When working out the size of an interval, start with the lower note and imagine that it is the tonic of a major key. Call this note 1, and then count up the notes of the major scale until you arrive at the upper note.

Look at the interval marked **1** at the start of Example 1.9 *below*. The lower note is C, so count up a scale of C major until you arrive at the upper note (F). You should have counted four notes (C D E F). This interval is therefore a 4th.

Now look at the interval marked **2**. This time the higher note comes first, but you should still calculate the interval from its lower note (F). Count up a scale of F major until you arrive at the upper note (A). You will have counted three notes (F G A), so this interval is a 3rd. We can be more precise. Because the note A is note 3 in the major scale of F, we can describe it as a **major 3rd**.

Next look at the interval marked **3**. The lower note is E, so you need to count up the scale of E major – E F♯ G♯. The note in our interval is G, not G♯ – it is a semitone lower than note 3 of E major and we therefore describe it as a **minor 3rd**.

Finally, look at the interval marked **4**. Is this is a major 3rd or a minor 3rd?

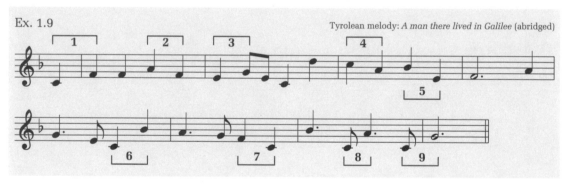

Ex. 1.9   Tyrolean melody: *A man there lived in Galilee* (abridged)

The large interval between C and D at the end of the second complete bar is a 9th (the nine notes are C D E F G A B C D). A 9th is an octave (8th) plus a 2nd. Yes, 8+2 really does make 9 in this case, because one note is counted twice when the two parts of the interval are calculated separately (C D E F G A B♭ C = 8; C D = 2).

Intervals larger than an octave are often termed **compound intervals**. Although we often speak of 9ths and 10ths, a 9th can be called a compound 2nd (or just a 2nd for short), and a 10th can be called a compound 3rd (or just a 3rd). 11ths, 12ths, 13ths, and so on are usually referred to as compound 4ths, 5ths, 6ths, etc. – or just as 4ths, 5ths, 6ths.

Activity 1.9

(a) Look again at Example 1.9. Play or sing it, and count the other intervals. Explain the differences in musical effect between the small intervals and the larger ones.

(b) Count intervals from other melodies until this activity becomes second nature. You can use other melodies from this book, or perhaps from set works that you are studying.

1.10 Naming intervals by type

Numbering intervals by counting letter names allows us to tell the difference between 2nds, 3rds, 4ths and so on. But as we saw when we looked at intervals **2** and **3** in the previous example, there can be two types of 3rd – major or minor. Intervals of a 2nd, 6th and 7th also come in major and minor varieties.

When referring to the type of interval it is important to realise that 'major' means greater and 'minor' means lesser – a minor interval is always a semitone smaller than a major interval. This use of 'major' and 'minor' is nothing to do with the key of the music – tunes usually include both major and minor intervals, whatever their key.

4th, 5ths and 8ths don't have major and minor versions. They are known as perfect intervals or, in the case of the 8th, simply as an octave.

Ex. 1.10

Two other types of interval you need to know about are shown in Example 1.10. The lower note of the first is D. Count up the scale of D major and you will find that A is the fifth note. However, the note here is A♭ so this interval is not a perfect 5th. It is one semitone smaller than a perfect 5th and is known as a **diminished 5th**.

The lower note of the second interval in Example 1.10 is A♭. Count up the scale of A♭ major and you will find that D♭ is the fourth note. However, the note here is D(♮) so this interval is not a perfect 4th. It is one semitone larger than a perfect 4th and is known as an **augmented 4th**.

1.11 Table of intervals

Here are the most common types of interval, up to an octave. For information, the number of semitone steps in each interval is shown in column two, while column three gives an example of each when C is the lower note.

Interval	Number of semitone steps	Example
minor 2nd	1 (a semitone)	C–D♭
major 2nd	2 (a tone)	C–D
minor 3rd	3	C–E♭
major 3rd	4	C–E
perfect 4th	5	C–F
augmented 4th	6 *	C–F♯
diminished 5th	6 *	C–G♭
perfect 5th	7	C–G
minor 6th	8	C–A♭
major 6th	9	C–A
minor 7th	10	C–B♭
major 7th	11	C–B
(perfect) octave	12	C–C an octave above

*   An augmented 4th and a diminished 5th have the same number of semitones and therefore are of the same size, but in context each has a different effect.

Activity 1.11.1

(a) Give the full description (for example minor 6th or augmented 4th) of each of the intervals marked **5–9** in Example 1.9, *opposite*.

(b) Which four intervals in the table above do not occur anywhere in Example 1.9?

To learn the characteristic sounds of the intervals shown in the table on the previous page:

✦ Play each interval – both ascending (as shown in column three) and descending

✦ Sing each interval – both descending and ascending

✦ Get someone to test you by playing you random selections of intervals

✦ Sing or play melodies which begin with, or include, particular types of intervals (for example, *Morning has broken* begins with major 3rd, minor 3rd and perfect 4th, together spanning an octave and making a broken chord or arpeggio).

1.12 How to identify any interval

The table in section 1.11 listed only the most common intervals, but the principles we have learnt can easily be extended to include identifying *any* interval:

1 Imagine that the lower note of the interval is the tonic of a major scale.

2 Count from this note to the upper note (e.g. D to F♯ is a 3rd, G to E♭ is a 6th).

3 Find out whether or not the upper note belongs to the major scale of which the lower note is the tonic.

4a If it does:

   ✦ a 2nd or a 3rd is major
   ✦ a 4th or a 5th is perfect
   ✦ a 6th or a 7th is major
   ✦ an octave is perfect

4b If it does not, the interval is:

   ✦ minor   if it is a semitone smaller   than a major interval
   ✦ diminished   if it is a semitone smaller   than a perfect or minor interval
   ✦ augmented   if it is a semitone larger   than a perfect or major interval

Look at the following melody and play it through:

Ex. 1.12.1

Bach: *Magnificat*

To identify interval **1** in this example:

✦ Start from the *lower* note (E) and count up the scale of E major.

✦ Note 2 of E major is F♯, so this is some kind of 2nd.

✦ E–F♯ would be a major second, but the upper note in our interval is F(♮), a semitone below F♯. The interval is a semitone smaller than a major 2nd – it must therefore be a **minor 2nd.** Remember: 'the interval is minor if it is a semitone smaller than a major interval'.

Interval **2** is a 6th. Because G is the lower note, think in terms of the G major scale. Does this scale have an E? Yes. So this interval is a **major 6th.**

Now look at interval **3**. As always, remember to count from the lower note (B♭). The scale of B♭ major has C as its second note, so B♭–C would be a major 2nd. The interval here (B♭–C♯) is a semitone larger, so this interval is an **augmented 2nd**.

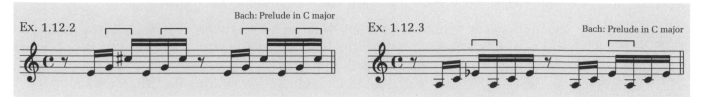

Ex. 1.12.2   Bach: Prelude in C major   Ex. 1.12.3   Bach: Prelude in C major

In Example 1.12.2 every bracketed interval is the same because the effect of the sharp lasts throughout the bar. G to C would be an interval of a perfect 4th, but here we have G to C♯, which is one semitone larger. It is therefore an **augmented 4th**.

Similarly, in Example 1.12.3, the effect of the E♭ lasts throughout the bar, so both bracketed intervals are the same. A to E would be a perfect 5th, but here we have A to E♭, which is one semitone smaller, making this a **diminished 5th**.

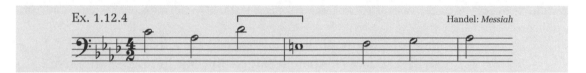

Ex. 1.12.4   Handel: *Messiah*

Finally, the bracketed interval in Example 1.12.4 is a **diminished 7th**. E♮ is the lower note (notice the music is in the bass clef). In key of E major, E–D♯ would be a major 7th. The interval a semitone smaller (E–D♮) would be a minor 7th. But our interval is a semitone smaller still. It must be diminished, because an 'interval is diminished if it is a semitone smaller than a minor interval'.

Activity 1.12

(a) Identify intervals **4** and **5** in Example 1.12.1, *opposite*.

(b) Identify intervals from as many other melodies in this book as possible.

(c) Using a treble stave and a key signature of G major, write the following pitches. They form the start of a well-known tune: try to add the rhythm if you can.

Begin with D (a tone above middle C) and repeat it.
Move up a major 2nd (to E), and then back to D.
Next go up a perfect 4th, and then down a minor 2nd.
Now go down a major 3rd and repeat this note.
Move up a major 2nd, down a major 2nd, up a perfect 5th and down a major 2nd.

1.13 Harmonic intervals

Ex. 1.13.1

Both notes are sounded together in harmonic intervals, but they are calculated and named in just the same way as melodic intervals, starting from the lower note. In Example 1.13.1, the first interval is a major 3rd and the second is a minor 3rd. Notice that the notes in harmonic intervals are sometimes written with a single stem and sometimes with separate stems in opposite directions.

Ex. 1.13.2

Example 1.13.2 shows an 'interval' we haven't mentioned before – two different parts playing or singing the same pitch. This is known as a **unison**. Notice that if the notes are semibreves there are no stems to point in different directions, so the semibreves are staggered. They should *just* touch.

Ex. 1.13.3

Staggered note-heads are also needed when writing a 2nd as a harmonic interval. Look carefully at Example 1.13.3. Stems always go between the two note-heads of a 2nd, whatever their direction. If accidentals are needed they are always written before the complete interval, with the lower one first if there are two.

Sometimes the notes in a harmonic interval are on different staves. The method is no different – just remember how the bass and treble staves overlap and count in the usual way. The first interval in Example 1.13.4 is a perfect 5th. The second interval is a unison, because both notes are middle C. Try naming the other intervals.

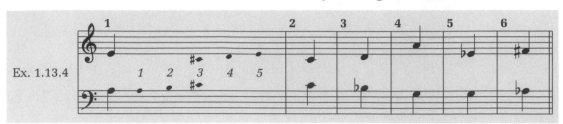

Ex. 1.13.4

Activity 1.13

Name the harmonic intervals **2–10** in the music below. Interval **1** is a minor 6th (G–E♭). Strictly, it is a compound minor 6th, but in practice the word 'compound' is usually dropped. Notice that new harmonic intervals can be created when a previous note hangs on, as shown by the lines in intervals **8** and **10**.

Vivaldi: Sonata in C minor

1.14 Writing intervals

The method for identifying intervals will work just as well if you have to write an interval *above* a given note. For instance, if you want to write a minor 3rd above G, count three notes up the scale of G major (to B). This will give you the major 3rd, so then lower the upper note by a semitone (to B♭) to form the minor 3rd.

If you want to write an interval *below* a given note, such as a major 3rd beneath G, first count down 3 letter names (G F E). Then, in the usual way, count 3 notes up the scale of E major to see if you arrive back on G. You don't! You arrive on G♯, a semitone too high. Since G is fixed, move the *lower* note down a semitone, to E♭. Confirm that this is right by counting up a scale of E♭ major to check that note 3 is G.

Activity 1.14

Add a note to each of the following to make the named harmonic intervals:

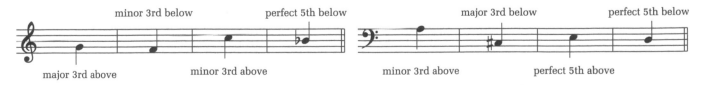

2 Chords

A chord is heard when two or more notes are sounded together.

Since about 1900 some composers have formed chords from almost any combination of notes. Before this, people generally relied on a smallish number of familiar chords, some of which are still widely used today, not least in popular music and film music. We need to learn about them to be able to harmonise chorales, complete baroque counterpoint exercises or add middle eights in 32-bar pop songs.

2.1 Triads

Ex. 2.1

The most widely used type of chord is the **triad**. The very word 'tri-ad' suggests that three notes are involved. However, a triad cannot be *any* combination of three notes. The triads in Example 2.1 contain two 3rds, one on top of the other. But we can also describe them like this:

✦ the top note is a 5th above the bottom note	bottom to top = 5
✦ the middle note is a 3rd above the bottom note	bottom to middle = 3

The chords in Example 2.1 are triads in their most basic form. When the intervals are a 3rd and a 5th above the bottom note, which is known as the root, the triad is said to be in **root position**, and can be described as a $\frac{5}{3}$ chord.

2.2 Types of triads

There are four types of $\frac{5}{3}$ chord – major, minor, diminished and augmented – although major and minor are by far the most common:

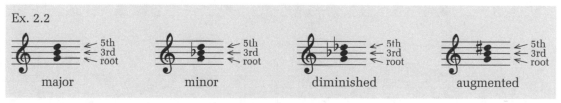

Ex. 2.2

major   minor   diminished   augmented

The root of a $\frac{5}{3}$ chord is its foundation and its most vital part. The middle note is called the 3rd because it is a 3rd above the root and the top note is called the 5th because it is a 5th above the root.

Every **major triad** has

- ✦ A *perfect* 5th between the root and the 5th
- ✦ A *major* 3rd between the root and the 3rd.

Every **minor triad** has

- ✦ A *perfect* 5th between the root and the 5th
- ✦ A *minor* 3rd between the root and the 3rd.

Every **diminished triad** has

- ✦ A *diminished* 5th between the root and the 5th
- ✦ A *minor* 3rd between the root and the 3rd.

Every **augmented triad** has

- ✦ An *augmented* 5th between the root and the 5th
- ✦ A *major* 3rd between the root and the 3rd.

Diminished and augmented triads are uncommon largely because their diminished and augmented 5ths make them sound less settled than major and minor $\frac{5}{3}$ chords.

A triad is usually referred to by its root note and type. So the four triads identified in Example 2.2 are G major, G minor, G diminished and G augmented.

To work out what notes belong to a particular major or minor $\frac{5}{3}$ chord, you need to know that:

✦ A major $\frac{5}{3}$ chord consists of notes 1, 3 and 5 of the *major* scale that starts on the root. For example, a triad of E♭ major consists of E♭ G B♭

✦ A minor $\frac{5}{3}$ chord consists of notes 1, 3 and 5 of the *minor* scale that starts on the root note. For example, a triad of F minor consists of F A♭ C.

After a while, you won't have to work each triad out from scratch every time. You'll begin to remember, for example, that an A major $\frac{5}{3}$ chord is A C♯ E.

Activity 2.2

(a) Play the four triads in Example 2.2 (on the previous page) as chords and then play them melodically (each note separately). Sing the melodic versions. Can you hear the differences between them?

(b) Ask someone to play some more triads so that you can get really good at spotting the different types.

(c) Identify the triads marked ∗ on staves (i) and (ii) *below*. In each case, label the root 'R', the 3rd '3' and the 5th '5'. For example, the first $\frac{5}{3}$ chord in (i) is F major, with F being 'R', A being '3' and C being '5'. Use your ears as well as your eyes!

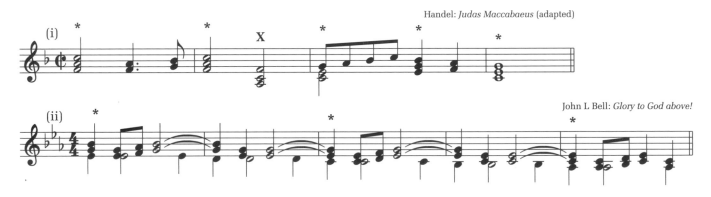

Handel: *Judas Maccabaeus* (adapted)

John L Bell: *Glory to God above!*

(d) Write the following *major* triads on a treble stave and label the notes R, 3 and 5: C, G, A, B♭, E, D, A♭.

(e) Write the following *minor* triads on a treble stave and label the notes R, 3 and 5: E, A, B, F, G, C, D.

2.3 Triads in first inversion

The triads discussed so far are said to be in **root position**, because the root is the lowest note. If you alter the order of the notes so that the root is no longer at the bottom, you create an **inversion**. Look at the chord marked **X** on stave (i) *above*. It is a chord of F major (F A C) but the lowest note is A, not F. It is an inverted chord.

Ex. 2.3.1

Now look at the first chord in Example 2.3.1, *left*. It is a G-major triad. If you juggle the notes so that the G flips up an octave, leaving B at the bottom, you have a triad of G major in **first inversion**.

The intervals in first-inversion chords follow this pattern:

✦ the top note is a 6th above the bottom note   bottom to top   = 6
✦ the middle note is a 3rd above the bottom note   bottom to middle   = 3

This explains why first inversions are referred to as $\frac{6}{3}$ chords. The first inversion chord in Example 2.3.1 consists of B D G. G is a 6th above B, and D is a 3rd above B.

The descriptions of the notes in a chord do not change when it is inverted. As you can see in Example 2.3.2, the root is still the root, the 3rd is still the 3rd, and the 5th is still the 5th. What is different is that **the root is no longer the lowest note when a chord is inverted**. Be very careful over this point.

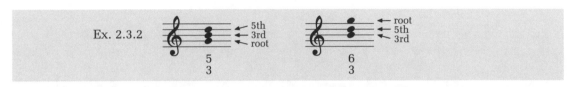

Ex. 2.3.2

Activity 2.3

(a) Play again the major and minor triads in Example 2.1 on page 19. Play them as chords and melodically (that is, with notes separately). Sing the melodic versions. Then play and sing the same chords as first inversions, again both as chords and melodically. Are you sure of the differences in sound between major and minor triads and the first inversions which contain the same notes?

(b) Ask someone to play more $\frac{5}{3}$ and $\frac{6}{3}$ chords so that you get really good at spotting the difference. Concentrate on majors and minors, with a few diminished.

(c) Find, and then name, each $\frac{6}{3}$ chord in the following quotation. Label the root 'R' in each case. For example, the first $\frac{6}{3}$ chord is the first inversion of C major in the second half of bar 1. Its root is C at the top of the chord.

Don't forget that this means
B is B♭ throughout the bar   Bernstein: *West Side Story* (upper parts)

(d) Write, on a treble stave, the following *major* triads in $\frac{6}{3}$ position and label the root as 'R' in each one. The answer to the first chord is: A C F (R=F).
F, D, A, B♭, E, A♭, E♭

(e) Identify the following major and minor triads in $\frac{6}{3}$ position and label the root as 'R' in each one. The answer to the first chord is given.

E minor

2.4 Triads in second inversion

Ex. 2.4.1

Earlier we juggled G B D so that it became B D G (see Example 2.3.1 on page 20).

Now continue juggling, so that the B of B D G flips up an octave to the top of the chord and D is at the bottom.

This creates a triad in **second inversion** (D G B), shown in Example 2.4.1, *left*.

The intervals in second-inversion chords follow this pattern:

✦ the top note is a 6th above the bottom note   bottom to top   = 6
✦ the middle note is a 4th above the bottom note   bottom to middle   = 4

This explains why second inversions are referred to as $\frac{6}{4}$ chords. The second inversion chord in Example 2.4.1 consists of D G B. B is a 6th above D, and G is a 4th above D.

Remember, the descriptions of the notes in a chord do not change when it is inverted. As you can see in Example 2.4.2, the root is still the root, the 3rd is still the 3rd, and the 5th is still the 5th:

Ex. 2.4.2

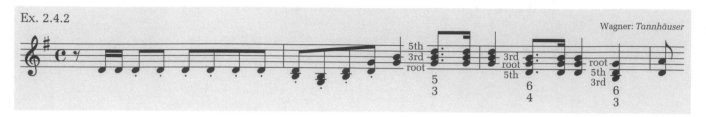

Wagner: *Tannhäuser*

Take careful note of this important tip.

$\frac{6}{4}$ chords are used *much* less frequently than $\frac{5}{3}$ and $\frac{6}{3}$ chords in the styles of music discussed in this book. Many of the mistakes in harmony and counterpoint exams arise from overuse of $\frac{6}{4}$ chords.

Activity 2.4

(a) Play again the major and minor triads in Example 2.1 on page 19. Play them as chords and melodically (that is, with notes separately). Sing the melodic versions. Then play and sing the same chords as second inversions, again both as chords and melodically. Are you sure of the differences in sound between major and minor triads and the second inversions which contain the same notes?

(b) Ask someone to play some more $\frac{5}{3}$, $\frac{6}{3}$ and $\frac{6}{4}$ chords so that you get really good at spotting the differences.

(c) Find, and then name, each $\frac{6}{4}$ chord in the following passage. Label the root 'R' in each case. The first answer has been given.

W P Rowlands: *Blaenwern* (adapted)

(d) Identify the following major and minor triads in $\frac{6}{4}$ position and label the root as 'R' in each one. The answer to the first chord is given.

Unsure of the answers to the last two chords? Check the table of more unusual keys on page 174.

(e) Write, on a *bass* stave, the following triads in $\frac{6}{4}$ position and label the root as 'R' in each one:

C major, D major, E♭ major, F minor, G minor, A major

2.5 Root-position triads in major keys

Triads do not exist in isolation. They exist within keys, which they help to establish and maintain.

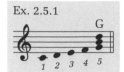
Ex. 2.5.1

Each triad in a key can be called by the name or number of the scale degree of its root. For instance, a D-major triad in the key of D major is the tonic triad because it has the tonic note of the key as its root. As shown in Example 2.5.1, a G-major triad in the key of C major is the dominant triad because it has the dominant note of the key as its root.

It is quicker to use numbers to identify triads. We employ roman numerals for this purpose instead of the arabic ('ordinary') numbers used for degrees of the scale. So chord I is another name for the tonic triad, chord V for the dominant triad, and so on. To put it another way, chord I has note 1 as its root, chord V is built on note 5, etc.

Chords can also be labelled with the symbols used in jazz and popular music:

✦ Major triads have the letter names of their roots
  ✦ Example: D means a D-major chord

✦ Minor triads have the letter names of their roots plus 'm' for minor
  ✦ Example: Em means an E-minor chord

✦ Diminished triads have the letter names of their roots plus 'dim' (or °)
  ✦ Example: E dim or E° means a diminished chord on E

✦ Augmented triads have the letter names of their roots plus 'aug' (or ⁺)
  ✦ Example: F aug or F⁺ means an augmented chord on F.

The following table gives the complete set of seven triads for the key of D major, one for each degree of the scale.

Note the following points, which apply to chords in *all* major keys:

✦ There are three major triads (I, IV and V). These are known as the **primary triads**. Two of them, I and V, are particularly important in establishing the key.

✦ There are three minor triads (ii, iii and vi) in every major key. Their numbers are printed in lower-case type to remind you that they are minor.

✦ The triad on the leading note (*vii*) is a diminished triad. The roman numerals of diminished chords are printed in lower-case *italic* type in this book.

Scale degree	Scale number	Chord number	Type of triad	Chord name and notes in D major			
Tonic	1	I	**major**	**D**	**D**	**F♯**	**A**
Supertonic	2	ii	minor	Em	E	G	B
Mediant	3	iii	minor	F♯m	F♯	A	C♯
Subdominant	4	IV	major	G	G	B	D
Dominant	5	V	**major**	**A**	**A**	**C♯**	**E**
Submediant	6	vi	minor	Bm	B	D	F♯
Leading note	7	*vii*	diminished	C♯dim	C♯	E	G

Here are examples of all seven chords in the key of D major:

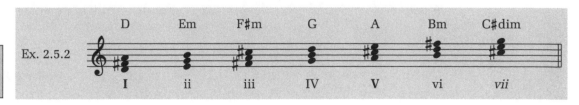
Ex. 2.5.2

(a) Write chord tables similar to the one on the previous page for at least four other major keys (for instance, C, F, G and B♭).

(b) On a treble stave, write triads I and V in C major, E♭ major, A major and B♭ major.

(c) On a bass stave, write triads I and V in F major, G major, D major and A♭ major.

(d) This is an exercise to help you think fairly quickly in a variety of keys. Begin by playing an F-major scale. Then play triads I, V and I again in F major. Next play a different major scale (perhaps G major) followed by triads I V I. Do the same in other major keys.

What you've just done is to **transpose** chords from one key to another. Such transposition is the best way of getting to understand the relationships between keys and chords.

2.6 First-inversion triads in major keys

You may also sometimes see first-inversion chords referred to in the style I⁶₃ or I⁶, etc.

Here are the triads of D major in first inversion. When using roman numerals, the letter 'b' is added to indicate a first inversion ($^6_3$) chord. (Technically, root-position chords are in position 'a' – Ia, Va and so forth – but the 'a' is not normally included). When using chord names, the lowest note of the chord is shown after a slash symbol if the chord is not in root position:

Ex. 2.6

(a) Write chord tables similar to the one on the previous page for first-inversion chords in at least four other major keys (for instance, C, F, G and B♭).

(b) On a treble stave, write chords Ib and Vb in the keys of C major, E♭ major, A major and B♭ major.

(c) On a bass stave, write chords Ib and Vb in the keys of F major, G major, D major and A♭ major.

(d) Here is another exercise in transposition. Begin by playing an F-major scale. Then play chords Ib, *viib*, Ib, iib in F major. Now play a different major scale (perhaps G major) followed by chords Ib, *viib*, Ib, iib. Do the same in other major keys.

2.7 Second-inversion triads in major keys

A letter 'c' is placed after the roman numeral to indicate a second-inversion chord. When using chord names, the lowest note is shown after a slash symbol if the chord is not in root position.

Ex. 2.7

Chord Ic (sometimes referred to as I$^6_4$) is the only $^6_4$ chord that we need to identify at present: it is shown in the key of D major in Example 2.7.

(a) Using a treble stave, write chord Ic in each of the following major keys: F, B♭, C, A, E, G.

(b) Identify the key and chord (including correct inversion) of each of the following tonic triads. They include chords I, Ib and Ic. The first answer is given.

Ic
C major

2.8 Root-position triads in minor keys

As you already know, minor scales are variable in a way that major scales are not. For example, scales of D minor always begin D E F G A – they may then have B♮ or B♭, and C or C♯.

Accordingly, no fewer than 13 triads are available in each minor key, because the chords that contain note 6 or note 7 (which means all chords except the tonic) exist in two different versions. For example in D minor, the chord on the second note of the scale (E) can be E G B (the minor triad ii) or E G B♭ (the diminished triad *ii*).

But when you come to work harmony exercises, you will more often than not use **chords based on the harmonic minor scale** – in D minor this means B♭ and C♯ rather than B♮ and C. In the following table, note that:

✦ Major triads occur in minor keys, just as minor triads occur in major keys

✦ The primary triads are i, iv and V, as they are in major keys, but notice that i and iv are minor, while V is major

✦ Once again, chords i and V are absolutely vital in establishing the key.

Scale degree	Scale number	Chord number	Type of triad	Chord name and notes in D minor		
Tonic	1	i	**minor**	**Dm**	**D**	**F**	**A**
Supertonic	2	ii	diminished	E dim	E	G	B♭
Mediant	3	*III*	augmented	F aug	F	A	C♯ *
Subdominant	4	iv	minor	G	G	B♭	D
Dominant	5	V	**major**	**A**	**A**	**C♯**	**E**
Submediant	6	VI	major	B♭	B♭	D	F
Leading note	7	*vii*	diminished	C♯dim	C♯	E	G

Here are examples of all seven chords in the key of D minor:

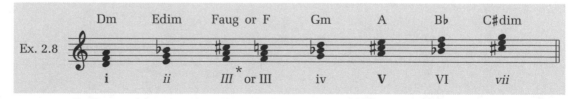

* The augmented version of the triad on the mediant is rare. The lowered version of note 7 is more commonly used in this chord, thus making it a major triad. For example, in the key of D minor, chord III is usually F A C rather than F A C♯.

Activity 2.8

(a) Write chord tables similar to the one on the previous page for at least four other minor keys (for instance, A minor, G minor, E minor, and C minor).

(b) On a treble stave, write chords i and V in the keys of A minor, C minor, F minor and F♯ minor. Remember to include all necessary accidentals.

(c) On a bass stave, write chords i and V in the keys of E minor, G minor, B minor and D minor. Remember to include all necessary accidentals.

(d) This is another exercise in transposition. Play the scale of A harmonic minor. Then play chords i, V and i in A minor. Next play a different minor scale (perhaps G minor) plus chords i, V and i in that key. Do the same in other minor keys.

2.9 First-inversion and second-inversion triads in minor keys

Here are the first-inversion triads in D minor. As we noted in the previous section, we will be using mainly chords based on the harmonic minor scale, but remember that the different possibilities for notes 6 and 7 in the minor scale mean that you will sometimes encounter various other versions of all chords except the tonic.

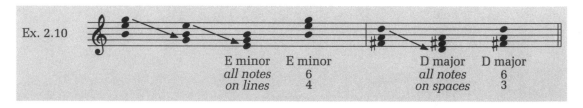

Chord Ic is the only second-inversion triad that we need to identify at present: it is shown in the key of D minor in Example 2.9.2.

2.10 Identifying inverted chords

To find the letter name of an inverted triad, keep moving its top note down an octave until the notes of the chord are *all* on either lines or spaces. This will give you the chord in root position, thus enabling you to name it:

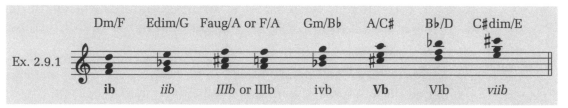

Activity 2.10

Label each of the following chords with a roman numeral and (where necessary) an inversion letter, and/or with the correct chord name (e.g. Gm/B♭). Keys are given.

2.11 Seventh chords

A $\frac{5}{3}$ contains two 3rds, one on top of the other. If we extend the pile of 3rds to three, we get a seventh chord, so called because there is an interval of a 7th between the root and the top note.

The intervals in seventh chords follow this pattern:

✦ the top note is a 7th above the root	bottom to top	= 7
✦ the second highest note is a 5th above the root	bottom to middle	= 5
✦ the second lowest note is a 3rd above the root	bottom to second lowest	= 3

Ex. 2.11.1

The seventh chord in Example 2.11.1 is A^7 (a chord of A major plus a 7th) and it consists of A, C♯ a 3rd higher, E a 3rd higher still, and G a 3rd higher again.

You can build a seventh chord by adding an additional 3rd above any root-position triad, but the two most common are those on notes 2 and 5 of the scale – the **supertonic 7th** and the **dominant 7th**. Here they are in the keys of D major and D minor:

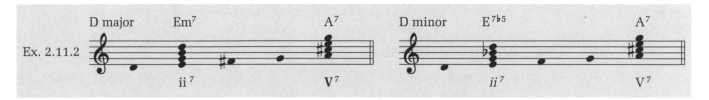

Ex. 2.11.2

There are several things to notice about these chords:

✦ Chord V^7 is exactly the same in the tonic minor as it is in the tonic major key

✦ The 7th in all four chords printed here is a *minor* 7th above the root

✦ The triads below each 7th are the same as those we learnt earlier – V is major, while ii is a minor triad in major keys, but a diminished triad in minor keys.

Diminished 7th chords will be discussed on the next page.

The '♭5' in the chord notation for $E^{7♭5}$ reflects the diminished 5th in the chord. This type of chord is sometimes called a 'half-diminished 7th' – half, because the 5th is diminished but the 7th is not. You may sometimes see the chord notated as $E^{\emptyset}$.

Activity 2.11

(a) On a treble stave write chords ii^7 and V^7 in the following keys:
C major, E♭ major, A minor and F minor.

(b) On a bass stave write chords ii^7 and V^7 in the following keys:
G major, B♭ major, E minor and C minor.

2.12 Inverting seventh chords

Seventh chords are inverted in exactly the same way as triads but, because they have four notes, there are *three* possible inversions instead of two. V^7 may appear in any inversion, but ii^7 and ii^7 are most often seen in first inversion.

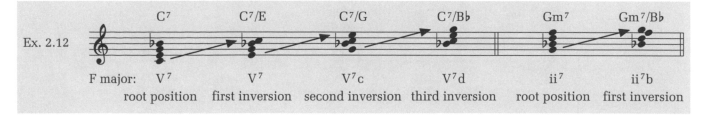

Ex. 2.12

To identify a seventh chord, use the method described in section **2.10** on page 26 – re-arrange the notes so they are *all* on either lines or spaces. This will give you the chord in root position, thus enabling you to name it.

Identify each of the following chords as either ii⁷ or V⁷ and indicate the inversion if the chord is not in root position. The first answer is given.

2.13 The diminished seventh

As mentioned in the previous section, seventh chords can be built on any note of the scale. The dominant 7th and supertonic 7th are the most common, but there is one other type you need to know about now, and that is the seventh chord on the leading note, chord *vii*⁷. Here it is in D minor, and then in D major:

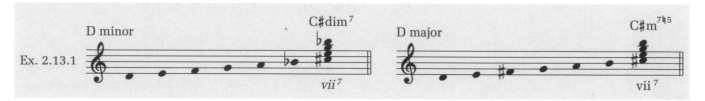

Let's look at the minor-key version first this time. In minor keys, chord *vii*⁷ is a diminished 7th – so called because there is an interval of a diminished 7th between the root and the upper note. It is easy to form a diminished 7th chord if you remember that each note is a minor 3rd higher than the previous one. You may sometimes see the chord symbol for a diminished 7th printed as °⁷ (for example, C♯°⁷).

In major keys, chord *vii*⁷ consists of two minor 3rds plus a *major* 3rd. This means that it includes the same diminished 5th between root and 5th as vii⁷ in a minor key, but the 7th itself is a *minor* 7th, not a diminished 7th, above the root. It is, in fact, the same type of half-diminished 7th that we saw on the previous page. Remember, you may see the chord name for the half-diminished 7th expressed in the form C♯ᵒ̷.

Example 2.13.2 shows the same two chords as Example 2.13.1, but an octave lower. To summarise the difference between diminished and half-diminished 7th chords:

✦ A **diminished 7th** consists of a minor 3rd, diminished 5th and diminished 7th above the root

✦ A **half-diminished 7th** consists of a minor 3rd, diminished 5th and minor 7th above the root.

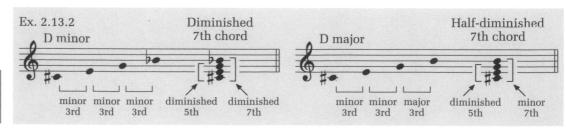

Write the chord indicated *above* each of the following notes. A tip: in this exercise, the note of each chord should either be all on lines or else all on spaces since every chord is in root position. Remember to play everything you write, either as a complete chord or by sounding the notes melodically.

| Dim7 | Dim7 | Half-dim7 | | Dim7 | Dim7 | Half-dim7 |

2.14 Chords in open position

So far we have kept the notes of each chord as close together as possible (in what is called **close position**). It is time now to find out how to spread the notes of a chord out over a wider range (in **open position**).

To do this, notes can be moved up or down by one or more octaves, and the order of the upper notes can be changed. But there is one vital rule:

✦ **The lowest note of the chord**, whether it is root, 3rd, 5th or 7th, **must always remain the lowest note**.

Here is a triad of F major, first in close position and then in various open spacings. Notice that the lowest note is always F, whatever the order of the upper notes.

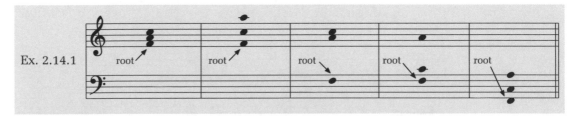

This principle holds good for inversions. The first stave in Example 2.14.2 shows a $\frac{6}{3}$ chord of F major in close position, followed by various open spacings. In each one, the 3rd (A) remains the lowest note.

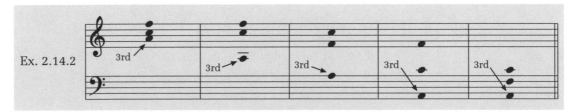

And the same principle applies to other chords, such as $\frac{6}{4}$ and seventh chords, and their various inversions. Here are a few examples:

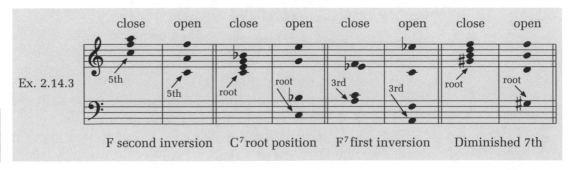

F second inversion   C⁷ root position   F⁷ first inversion   Diminished 7th

Despite all these different possibilities, the method for identifying chords in open position is very similar to the way we learnt earlier:

✦ Re-arrange the chord so that it is in close position and with all its notes on either lines or on spaces. The chord is then in *root position* and can be named.

Ex. 2.14.4

✦ From this, you can work out if the original chord is in root position or which inversion it is in.

This method is illustrated in Example 2.14.4. The first chord has been re-arranged into close position, with all notes on lines, by moving the bass-clef E♭ up an octave. This allows us to see that the chord is Cm⁷. In the original chord, the 3rd (E♭) is in the bass, so we can now say that it is Cm⁷ in first inversion.

Activity 2.14

(a) On a pair of staves (treble and bass) write two different open-position spacings for the root-position triads of E minor and G major. You can space your chords as you wish, but avoid too much use of leger lines. Then write two open-position spacings for the first and second inversions of the same chords.

(b) On a similar pair of staves, write two different open-position spacings of each of the following chords:
G⁷ in root position, first inversion and third inversion,
Dm⁷ in root position and first inversion.

(c) Fully identify each of the chords below. If you use roman numerals, add a letter to show any inverted chords. If you use chord names, show any inversions with 'slash chord' notation (for example, Cm/G). The key is G minor – remember that the key signature tells you that every B and every E is a flat.

2.15 Doubling and omitting notes

In order to lay out the notes of chords in the best way for voices or for different types of instrument, it is often necessary to omit a note of a chord (usually the 5th) and/or to **double** a note.

Doubling means using the same pitch in more than one part – either exactly the same pitch (unison) or the same pitch but in a different octave.

Example 2.15 on the next page contains a short passage in three parts (that is, with three simultaneous melodic lines). Chord 3 is a complete triad in close position, but some of the other chords include doubed notes, which means that one or more notes in the chord have to be omitted.

Look at chord 1 in the example. It has two Cs and an E – this is perfectly satisfactory since we still hear this as a C-major chord, despite there being no G. Chord 14 has a G all three parts. In the context this still implies a chord of G major, despite the absence of both B and D. We can say that chord 14 *implies* (rather than actually states) a triad of G major. Similarly, chord 1 implies, rather than states, a triad of C major.

Ex. 2.15   Purcell: *Dido and Aeneas* (adapted)

The following table identifies the first seven chords in this music, and shows which have doubled and omitted notes.

Number	Chord and position		Doublings and omissions
1	C	root position	root (C) doubled, 5th (G) omitted
2	Am	first inversion	3rd (C) doubled, 5th (A) omitted
3	G	root position	
4	G	root position	root (G) doubled, 5th (D) omitted
5	C	root position	
6	Am	root position	root (A) doubled, 5th (E) omitted
7	D	root position	

Activity 2.15

Write a table similar to the one above to identify the triads, inversions, doublings and omitted notes in chords 8–14 of the music at the top of this page.

2.16 Doubling notes in four-part writing

A great deal of music is written in four parts, including chorales harmonised by Bach, much other music for choirs, and quartets of various kinds. Even some orchestral writing is basically in four parts, with various instruments doubling some or all of these basic four parts.

Ex. 2.16

In four-part music, one note of a triad has to be doubled to make the fourth note. For instance, you might have C C G E rather than C E G, as shown in Example 2.16.

As we noted previously, the parts which create the doubling may play or sing in unison or may be one, two or more octaves apart.

There is more on doubling in Chapter 6. For the present, let's keep it simple – just remember that:

✦ In $\frac{5}{3}$ chords, the root is most commonly doubled

✦ In $\frac{6}{3}$ chords, there is greater variety (but composers avoid doubling note 7 of the scale, the leading note)

✦ In $\frac{6}{4}$ chords, the 5th (which is also the bass note) is usually doubled.

Seventh chords have four notes and therefore doubling is not always necessary in four-part writing. However, composers sometimes omit the 5th of seventh chords in root position, and double the root. Inversions of seventh chords rarely involve doubling or omitted notes.

Study the following quotation from a piano piece by Schumann. The key is G major and the music is in four parts. Even where there are only three notes, as in the first chord, Schumann thinks in terms of two notes in the right hand and two in the left, which is why there are two stems on the note in the left hand.

Schumann: *Choral* (adapted)

(a) Below the bass stave, label each chord with a roman numeral and, if necessary, a letter to show its inversion. The first answer is given.

(b) Show which note of each chord has been doubled by writing R, 3rd or 5th above the treble stave. There are two chords without doubled notes. Why is this?

2.17 Additional harmony notes

In two-part music, triads and seventh chords can only ever be implied, because at least one note is always omitted

However, you can sometimes give an impression of fuller harmony by using two or more different notes from the same chord in succession in one part, against a single note in another part. These extra notes are called **additional harmony notes**, and they are marked * in Example 2.17. They are useful in all kinds of music, however many parts it is in.

Corelli: Violin Sonata, Op 5 no 7

Ex. 2.17

The following passage is in F major. Write the correct chord symbol at each of the places marked * and draw a circle round all additional harmony notes.

Mozart: *Menuett* K 2 (adapted)

3   Chord progressions

3.1   What are chord progressions?

Any two or more chords heard in succession can be called a harmonic progression but the term **chord progression** is often used to describe particular successions of chords that have become regular, even standard, parts of our harmonic vocabulary.

Knowing about chord progressions will help you

✦ Choose chords when harmonising the chorale melodies in Chapter 6
✦ Understand the harmony of baroque counterpoint in Chapter 7
✦ Choose chords for the middle eights of 32-bar pop songs in Chapter 8
✦ Compose and analyse music
✦ Understand better the pieces you play or sing.

3.2   Functional harmony

From about 1680 until well into the 19th century (and in much later music as well) harmony was **functional** – that is, an important function or purpose of the chord progressions used was to establish and maintain a key.

Before seeing in detail how chord progressions work, we need to divide individual chords into three main groups according to their functions:

Ex. 3.2
C major
V   V⁷   vii
C major
ii   ii⁷   IV

✦ **The tonic group**: chord I and occasional alternatives, notably VI. Chord I has the tonic of the scale as its root, and is normally the only chord considered stable enough for a whole piece to end on.

✦ **The dominant group**: chord V, chord V^7, and chord VII (normally used in first inversion, as VIIb). The close relationship between these three chords is shown in Example 3.2. They all contain note 7, which has a powerful tendency to rise to 8, hence the name 'leading note'. It quite literally leads back to the upper tonic and so to the tonic group of chords.

✦ **The subdominant group**: the subdominant chord IV, plus chords II and II^7. The close relationship between these three chords is also shown in Example 3.2.

3.3   Chords I and V

Chords I and V (or V^7) are the two chords best able to establish and maintain a key, and much music (particularly in the 18th century) makes extensive use of them. Composers often move from I to $V^{(7)}$ (including their inversions) and from $V^{(7)}$ to I. This progression is not limited to 18th-century music, as you can see in this hit tune from the 1925 Broadway show, *No, No, Nanette*:

Ex. 3.3.1

Vincent Youmans: *I Want to be Happy*

C   G⁷

I want   to   be   hap - py,   but   I   won't   be   hap - py

G⁷   C

'til   I   make   you   hap - py   too. _____

Here is the same progression from a piece written by Mozart some 150 years earlier. The key is B♭ major and the chords are inverted, but the harmonic progression is otherwise identical.

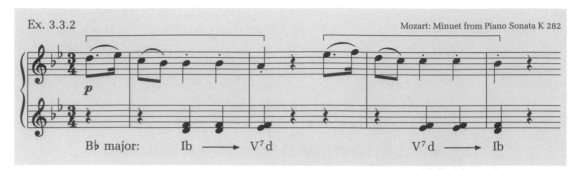

Play this example and notice the way in which the first phrase (marked with a bracket) is followed by a second phrase (also bracketed) of the same length. This aurally satisfying type of construction is often called a **question and answer**.

In Example 3.3.2 the first phrase sounds questioning because it invites more – it ends with the leading note in the melody, supported by (an incomplete) chord of V^7d, both sounding unfinished. The second phrase sounds like an answer, because the harmony resolves onto the tonic chord (Ib) and the melody returns to the tonic note. The two phrases are united by their identical length and, in this case, their identical rhythm.

It is often useful to think of chords I and $V^{(7)}$ as 'home and away' – chord I invites a journey away, while chord $V^{(7)}$ signals a need to return home.

3.4 The progression V–I

Chords V–I *in that order* make the strongest of all progressions – strong enough even to bring an entire section or piece to a convincing end.

The progression V–I includes movement from the leading note (7) in chord V to the upper tonic (8) in chord I. The leading note has a strong urge to move to the tonic. Try singing or playing a scale and stopping on note 7!

Example 3.4.1 shows a phrase from a major-key hymn tune in which chords V–I are used twice. If it helps, play just the outer parts, soprano and bass. Example 3.4.2 is an extract from a chorus by Purcell. Chords V–I appear three times in C minor and then twice in E♭, the relative major.

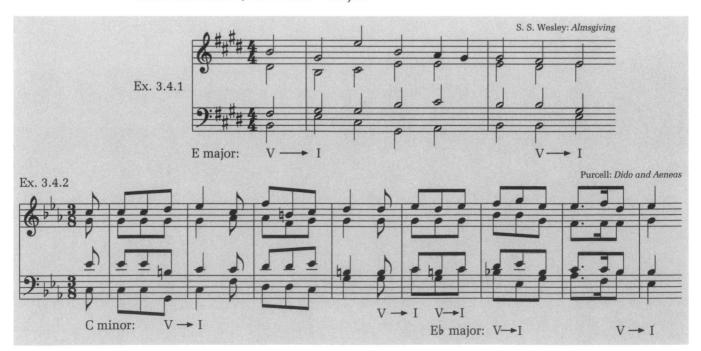

Mark examples of the progression V–I in the following extract.

William Croft (attributed): *Hanover* (adapted)

G major: iib

3.5 Perfect cadences

Both musical examples in section **3.4** finish with the progression V–I. The two chords that end a phrase are known as a **cadence**. The chord(s) immediately before the cadence itself are often regarded as part of the complete cadential progression.

The V–I cadence is a **perfect cadence**. In functional harmony it is by far the most widely-used type of cadence.

The adjective 'perfect' comes from a Latin word meaning finished or complete, but in practice not all perfect cadences are equally final. It depends partly on how final-sounding the melody is. If the tune ends with notes 2–1 or 7–8, the effect is likely to be more final than with, for example 5–3.

The bass in a perfect cadence can either descend from note 5 to note 1, as it does at the end of Example 3.4.2 *opposite*, or it can rise from note 5 to note 8 (the upper tonic) as it does at the end of Example 3.4.1 *opposite*. The descent of the bass from V to I, beneath a melody that ascends from note 7 to note 8, provides the most definitive type of perfect cadence, especially if the first chord is V^7 rather than just V:

Ex. 3.5

C major: V^7 I

Chord *viib* sometimes substitutes for $V^{(7)}$ in perfect cadences, although the effect is not as strong: for an example, see the chord marked ∗ in Activity **3.17**(a) on page 46.

Look for, and listen to, more examples of perfect cadences. Look (for instance) at Chapters 6 and 7, and more or less any other 18th-century music.

3.6 Approaching a perfect cadence

Look at the perfect cadence in bars 3–4 of Activity **3.4** at the top of this page. It is preceded by chord iib, which is one of the subdominant group of chords. In fact, any of the chords from that group makes an effective approach to a perfect cadence.

Many phrases that conclude with a perfect cadence end with the following three chords:

✦ A chord from the subdominant group, then
✦ A chord from the dominant group (usually V or V⁷), and finally
✦ Chord I from the tonic group.

Here are two more examples, one in A minor and the other in G major:

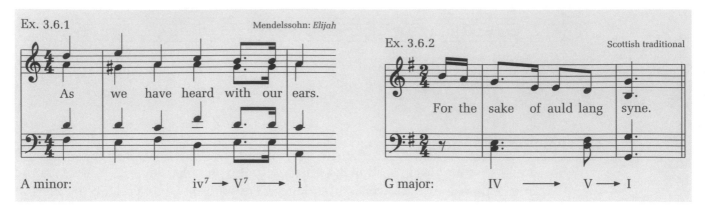

Activity 3.6

Here are the final phrases from four Christmas carols, all ending on the tonic. Name the key of each and add chord symbols at the places marked ∗, choosing an approach chord from the subdominant group followed by a perfect cadence in every case.

3.7 The cadential $^6_4$

The perfect cadence can also be approached from chord Ic. Although this is a very common approach, Ic is not really a fully independent chord but more a decoration of chord V, with which it shares the same bass note. For that reason, Ic is often used between an approach chord from the subdominant group and the actual perfect cadence, in such patterns as IV–Ic–V$^{(7)}$–I:

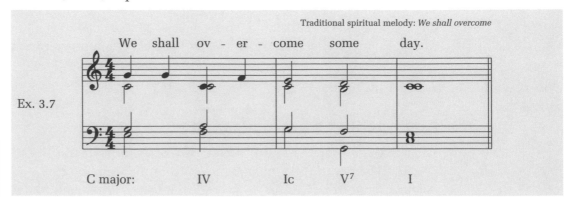

In Example 3.7, notice how

✦ E in chord Ic moves down by step to D in chord V
✦ C in chord Ic moves down by step to B in chord V
✦ Both chords have G in the bass.

In terms of intervals above the bass, we hear a 6th falling to a 5th, and a 4th falling to a 3rd. This $\frac{6}{4}$ – $\frac{5}{3}$ movement is the essence of the Ic–V progression. When chord Ic is used in this cadential position it is often called the **cadential $\frac{6}{4}$**.

Activity 3.7

Add notes on the treble stave of these two passages to complete chords Ic and V in the places indicated. Each chord requires two more notes. Check that the notes in each of your $\frac{6}{4}$ chords fall by step to the following $\frac{5}{3}$ chord, then play both phrases.

G major: vi   iib   Ic   V   I

F major: Ib   ii   Ic   V   I

3.8 Interrupted cadences

If you replace chord I in a perfect cadence with some other chord, you create an **interrupted cadence** – so called because it interrupts the expected progress of the music to the tonic. It is sometime used as a 'delaying tactic', creating the expectation that a perfect cadence will soon follow, as in Example 3.8.

Ex. 3.8   Handel: *Water music (adapted)*

G major: ivb → Ic → V → vi   ivb → Ic → V → I
           Interrupted   **Perfect**

Interrupted cadences frequently end with chord VI, as here, but any chord that creates an effective surprise (for example IVb) is possible. In a minor key, chord VI is major, which makes the effect of an interrupted cadence more arresting. Mozart's Requiem (a large-scale work for singers and orchestra) ends with the magnificent effect of a diminished 7th used as the second chord of an interrupted cadence – but after a silence, the expected perfect cadence follows to conclude the work.

Chord VI cannot replace I at a final cadence and it doesn't usually replace the tonic chord at the start of a piece either, because it is not very helpful in establishing the key. Whether or not VI is a suitable alternative to I in mid-phrase will depend on the context. In general, remember that interrupted cadences are *far* less common than perfect cadences.

(a) Here is the ending of a well-known piece, with the last chord missing. Label the three printed chords and then play the passage with a tonic chord at the end, to make a perfect cadence. Then try ending on chord vi to create an interrupted cadence. Note the difference.

G major:

Next, see if you can play the passage in G *minor*, still with an interrupted cadence (the final chord should be E♭ major).

Finally try ending on a diminished 7th, for a really surprising interruption!

(b) Name the key, label all the chords and identify both of the cadences indicated by brackets in these two final phrases from a well-known Christmas carol.

Melody by Franz Grüber: *Silent night*

3.9 Imperfect cadences

The progression I–V can be used almost anywhere – at the beginning, in the middle, or at the end of a phrase. At the end of a phrase it forms an **imperfect cadence**.

Imperfect cadences sound far less final than perfect cadences – ending on chord V leaves the music open to continue, not least since chord V includes the leading note (note 7) that has not yet fulfilled its destiny of rising to note 8. The adjective 'imperfect' comes from a Latin word meaning incomplete.

Example 3.9.1 contains two I–V progressions, the second of which creates an imperfect cadence.

Ex: 3.9.1

W H Havergal: *Franconia*

D major: I ⟶ V   I ⟶ V

Imperfect cadences must end with chord V, but they need not have I as the first chord. For example, many imperfect cadences consist of the progression ii–V or variants such as iib–V and ii^{7}b–V.

Chord V is often preceded by a cadential $\frac{6}{4}$ (chord Ic) in imperfect cadences, just as it is in perfect cadences, particularly in music of the classical period:

Ex: 3.9.2   Haydn: *The Creation*

C major: ii → Ic → V

Activity 3.9

Play each of the following. In each case identify the key and the chords marked *, and identify the cadences formed by these chords.

Hill: *Happy Birthday to You!*

Mozart: *The Magic Flute*

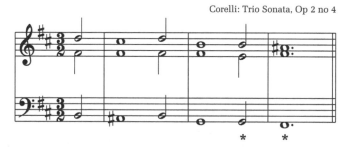

Corelli: Trio Sonata, Op 2 no 4

3.10 Plagal cadences

Ex. 3.10

A - men

A major: IV   I

The subdominant chord (IV) is widely used before and after I. Chords IV–I, when used at the end of phrase, make a **plagal cadence**.

A plagal cadence, like a perfect cadence, can end a section or piece, because its final chord is I, although it is used *far* less frequently than the perfect cadence.

Years ago it was common in church to sing 'Amen' to a plagal cadence at the end of a hymn and for this reason, people still occasionally call it an 'Amen' cadence.

3.11 Cadence summary

Here is a summary of the four cadences we have studied. Remember that perfect and imperfect cadences are used far more frequently than the other two types.

✦ Perfect: $V^{(7)}$ to I

✦ Imperfect: any chord to V (often $iib^{(7)}$–V)

✦ Interrupted: $V^{(7)}$ to any chord except I (often $V^{(7)}$–vi)

✦ Plagal: IV to I.

Chord progressions **39**

Study this hymn and then

(i)   Name the keys in the three places indicated

(ii) Identify each of the cadences marked with a bracket

(iii) Label the approach chords marked ∗.

Remember to think in terms of the new key in bars 9–12.

Melody by H J Gauntlett: *Laudate Dominum*

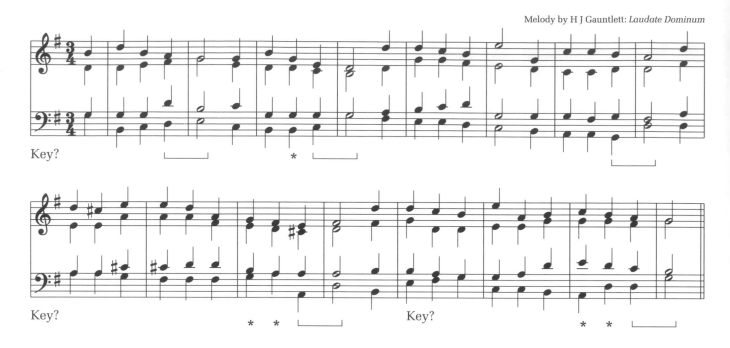

3.12 The circle of 5ths

Movement from V to I is so strong largely because of the downward leap of a 5th between the roots of the two chords. Other progressions with roots that fall a 5th (including I–IV) possess something of the same strength.

In practice 'down a 5th' can also mean 'up a 4th', since exactly the same pitches are involved. Look back at the V–I progressions you found in Activity **3.4** (page 35) – in the first and third, the bass rises from D to G, while in the second it falls from D to the G below, and yet the chord progressions are all V–I.

If you start on chord I and keep moving down in 5ths or up in 4ths, you will eventually return to the tonic chord and have an important and useful chord progression called the **circle of 5ths**. Ascending 4ths usually alternate with descending 5ths in a circle of 5ths so that the bass part doesn't descend into an impossibly low region:

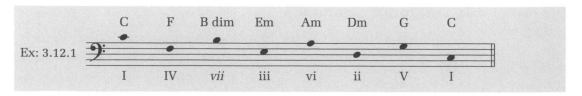

Notice that the interval between the second and third roots in this example is an augmented 4th (it would be a diminished 5th if the bass fell from F to the B below). While it is possible to move only in perfect 4ths and perfect 5ths it would take twelve moves to come full circle rather than seven and is something almost never done.

Even the seven-chord circle of 5ths is not often used in full, although here in outline is an example from a 1954 hit made famous by Frank Sinatra. Notice that this time the circle begins and ends on a chord of A minor.

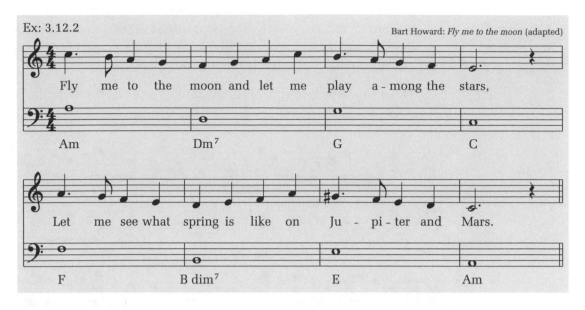

This example, like a few later ones in the chapter, includes some notes in the tune that are not in the underlying chords. We will learn about these in the next chapter, but for now just be aware that they don't alter the basic harmony.

References such as bar 4[1] mean bar 4, beat 1.

More typically, composers tend to use smaller segments from the circle of 5ths, such as the chord progression vi–ii–V–I. You can see an example in bars 3–4[1] of the music at the top of page 35 (chord ii is inverted here to provide a smoother bass part).

3.13 Harmonic sequences

Look at Example 3.12.2 *above* and compare bars 5–8 with the first four bars. Do you see that the tune is similar, except that it is two notes lower? This is known as a **melodic sequence**.

The chords also follow a similar pattern – the pattern of roots descending by 5ths and rising by 4ths in bars 1–4 is repeated in bars 5–8, but two notes lower. A chord progression repeated at a different pitch is called an **harmonic sequence**, and will usually accompany a melodic sequence, as it does here.

Circles of 5ths usually generate harmonic sequences of this kind, but it is also possible to create them with other chord progressions. In Example 3.13 the sequences are formed from repeated pairs of chords with roots that fall a 4th. Each repetition of the pattern is a 3rd lower than the previous one, giving the progression:

✦ I–V–I–V, vi–iii–vi–iii, IV–I–IV–I.

Notice the appearance of chord iii in Example 3.13 – we haven't often encountered this rather rare triad before. It is often followed by chord vi or chord IV, as it is here. Look at bars 5[3]–6[1] of the music for Activity **3.11** on the opposite page and you will see iiib followed by IV (Bm/D – C in the key of G major).

= B♭ major

(a) In the example below, the melody consists of **broken chords**. That is, the notes of each chord are played individually in various patterns, sometimes leaping down by more than an octave to prevent the patterns becoming too predictable. This doesn't affect the harmony, though – just add together the notes of each broken chord to work out what it is, as shown *left*.

Label the chords in the following music, and show where the harmonic sequences occur by marking each one with a bracket.

Handel: Violin Sonata No 3

(b) Write in the three missing chords in this circle of 5ths in the key of D major:
D – G – C♯ dim – F♯m – .... – Em – .... – ....

3.14 Other effective chord progressions

In addition to chords whose roots fall in 5ths, the following progressions work well and are very useful:

✦ **Roots that rise by a 5th** (or fall by a 4th), such as IV–I.

✦ **Roots that rise by a 2nd**, such as V–VI and I–II.

✦ **Roots that fall by a 3rd**, such as I down to VI, VI–IV, and IV–II. When strung together the first two progressions form the start of the chord pattern I–VI–IV–V, a favourite of generations of would-be pianists:

Ex: 3.14

C major: I   vi   IV   V

This is sometimes called the 'doo-wop' progression, because of its frequent use in the style of 1950s' pop known as doo-wop. A similar 'falling 3rds' progression is I–VI–IV–II–V–I, often used in early rock and roll. Both tended to be over-used and can (like the circle of 5ths) sound something of a cliché. However, stock progressions such as these are a good way of learning about harmony, especially if you try improvising around them in different keys.

We can summarise all of our work on progressions with the following rule of thumb: good progressions can generally be formed from chords that have roots which go

> ✦ **Up a 2nd, down a 3rd, up a 4th or down a 5th**
> *except* that V or vii should not be followed by chord iii at the end of a phrase.

3.15 Pedals

When composers want to emphasise the tonic or the dominant while creating additional harmonic interest and variety, they often use a **pedal**. This is a long sustained note (or successive repetitions of the same note) with changing harmonies going on around it.

The most common type is a **dominant pedal**. Typically it helps build a sense of expectation that chord I will arrive as a piece nears its end. The majority of pedals are in the bass, but they can occur at the top of the texture (an **inverted pedal**), or in an inner part (an **internal pedal**). In fact, Sullivan uses all three types in Example 3.15.1, although the inverted and internal pedals (also on G) have been omitted for clarity. This section of so-called 'dominant preparation' lasts for 19 bars in all, before one of the big tunes of the operetta returns in a triumphantly *ff* C major.

Ex: 3.15.1

Sullivan: *The Pirates of Penzance* (Overture)

A tonic pedal may be used at the beginning of a movement to help establish the key, as in Example 3.15.2, or at the end, to help being a piece to a satisfying and often peaceful conclusion.

Ex: 3.15.2

Bach: Prelude in C, BWV 939

When using a pedal, the surrounding harmony needs to form proper harmonic progressions, just as it would if the pedal wasn't there. As you can see above, the chords are identified just as they would be if there was no pedal.

3.16 Modulation

Modulation is the process of changing key. Changes of key provide welcome variety, and are valuable in terms of form and structure. Most pieces of any length move away from their starting key (the tonic) to one or more other keys and then return to the tonic before the end, as we saw in the music for Activity **3.11** on page 40.

Related keys

Modulations are most commonly to **related keys** – that is, to keys with the same signature as the tonic key, or with one more, or one fewer, sharps or flats. You may also encounter modulations between tonic minor and tonic major keys, for example from C minor to C major, or *vice versa*.

The following table shows these relationships for a piece in D major. In practice, most major-key works in the baroque and classical periods will modulate to the **dominant** at some point. Modulations to other related keys may or may not occur.

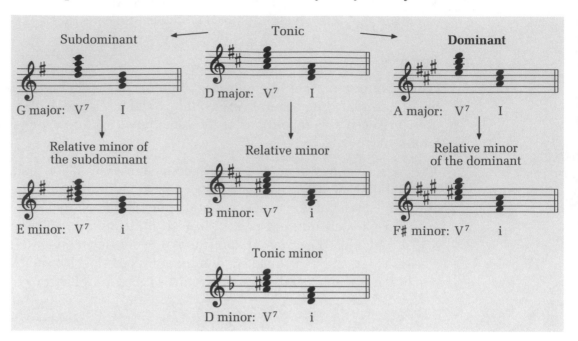

Chords V⁷ and I are shown in each key because these two chords are the main means by which a key is established. Notice that

✦ The relative minor has the same key signature as its relative major, but you need to sharpen note 7 in the minor key

✦ The dominant has one *more* sharp than the tonic, and you also need to sharpen note 7 in the relative minor of the dominant

✦ The subdominant has one *less* sharp than the tonic, but you also need to sharpen note 7 in the relative minor of the subdominant.

The same principles hold good for all keys – when you have no more sharps to take away you are in C major or A minor, so after that you need to add flats to keep going in a subdominant direction.

Here is a table of keys related to a minor key, using B minor as the example. In minor keys, a structurally-important modulation to the **relative major** is highly likely.

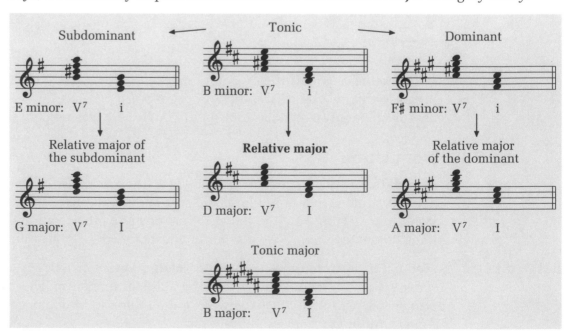

The tables *opposite* remind you of the key signatures for the various related keys. However, in practice there is not normally a change of key signature when music modulates (except occasionally for the change between tonic minor and tonic major).

Instead, you must use accidentals to represent the notes of the new key. This includes adding sharps or flats before individual notes to supplement those in the key signature, and/or adding naturals before individual notes to cancel sharps or flats present in the key signature.

This process needs great care, as it is easy to miss vital accidentals. You may find it helps to write out the note names of the new scale when music modulates.

3.17 How modulation works

The strongest of all chord progressions is V^7–I. Unlike a pair of chords such as Am and C, which can occur in several different keys, V^7–I can only ever occur in one key (the tonic). Consider G^7–C. This progression defines the key of C major because

✦ It contains F♮ so it cannot belong to a key with any sharps
✦ It contains B♮ so it cannot belong to a key with any flats
✦ It contains G♮ so it cannot belong to A minor, the only other key with no sharps or flats in its key signature.

The same holds good for V^7–I in any key, major or minor, making it the most decisive way to create a modulation and establish a new key. In Example 3.17.1 *below*:

✦ Phrase 1 is in F major and ends with an interrupted cadence in that key

✦ Phrase 2 is in F major and ends with an imperfect cadence in that key

✦ Phrase 3 modulates to the dominant key, which is confirmed by the definitive perfect cadence V^7–I in C major (G^7–C) at the end of this phrase

✦ Phrase 4 modulates back to the tonic key, which is confirmed by the definitive perfect cadence V^7–I in F major (C^7–F) at the end of this final phrase.

If the music modulates there will usually be a second modulation in order to return to the tonic key before the end (except in the case of short extracts used as examples, such as those on the next page). Even if there are modulations to several different keys in succession you should still normally expect the music to modulate back to the tonic for the final phrase(s) of the passage.

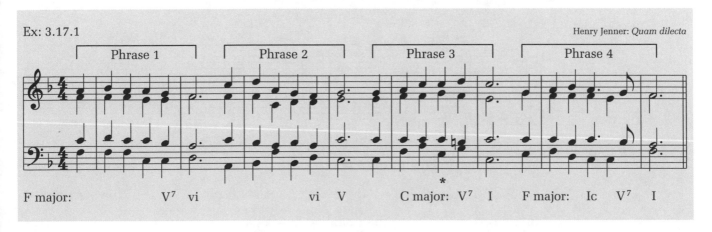

Ex: 3.17.1   Henry Jenner: *Quam dilecta*

F major: V^7 vi   vi   V   C major: V^7 I   F major: Ic V^7 I

The chord marked ∗ is Vb in F major, the key we are leaving, and Ib in C major, the key that is about to be established by the cadence at the end of phrase 3.

A chord that exists both in the old key and the new is called a **pivot chord** and it produces a particularly smooth transition to the new key. The same chord is used as a pivot back to F major at the start of phrase 4.

A pivot chord is not essential, but omitting it and plunging straight into a dominant 7th in the new key produces a much more abrupt modulation:

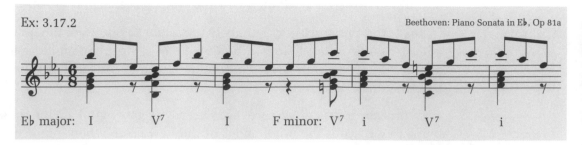

Ex: 3.17.2

Beethoven: Piano Sonata in E♭, Op 81a

E♭ major: I   V⁷   I   F minor: V⁷   i   V⁷   i

Activity 3.17

(a) Identify the three keys in the following passage by Handel:

Handel: *Acis and Galatea*

*

Notice the chord marked * in the final cadence of this passage. It is chord *viib* and is used as a subsitute for V⁽⁷⁾ in this perfect cadence.

(b) In the above passage, write Ic below the example of a cadential $\frac{6}{4}$.

(c) Study the modulation in the following passage, which includes a pivot chord indicated by a shaded box, and then complete the sentences below.

Bach: Minuet from French Suite No 3, BWV 814

This passage begins in the key of .... and ends in the key of

.... The pivot chord is chord .... in the starting key,

and chord .... in the final key of the passage.

(d) The progression shown *right* ends with an imperfect cadence. Add an accidental to make the chords modulate to the dominant instead.

3.18 Secondary dominants

Compare the following progressions:

Ex. 3.18.1

F major: Ib   iib   V   I   F major: Ib   *   V   I

The second is the same as the first, apart from the chord marked ∗. The B♮ in this cadence approach chord seems to be starting a modulation to C major, which is immediately aborted in favour of a perfect cadence in F major. In fact, there is no modulation – the approach chord in the second progression is a chromatic chord (that is, one outside of the current key) known as a **secondary dominant**.

A secondary dominant is the *major* chord a perfect 5th above any note of the scale except the tonic (because that would be the normal dominant chord) – although secondary dominants above the leading note are not used since they would be too remote from the current key.

Ex. 3.18.2

V of V   V   I

The chord marked ∗ in Example 3.18.1 is the first inversion of G major. This G-major triad acts as a temporary 'dominant' to the chord of C that follows it, as shown in Example 3.18.2. Note that there is **no modulation** because the cadence itself asserts the key of F major.

Here are the secondary dominants in the key of C major – they often include a minor 7th above the root, as shown in this example:

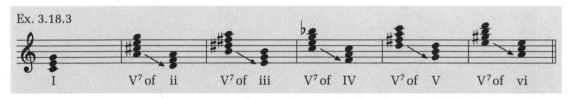

Ex. 3.18.3

I   V⁷ of ii   V⁷ of iii   V⁷ of IV   V⁷ of V   V⁷ of vi

The essence of secondary-7th progressions is again the strength of the falling 5th from the root of the chromatic chord to the root of the chord that follows. Instead of changing key, they serve to reinforce the importance of the chords onto which they fall.

Secondary 7ths are the most common type of chromatic chord and can lend colour to standard cadential progressions. Sometimes a whole series of them is used in succession, as in the next two examples.

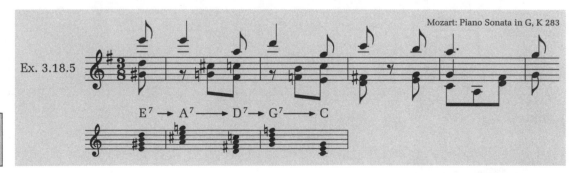

Ex. 3.18.4   Johnny Marks: *Rudolph the red-nosed reindeer*

G   E⁷ ⟶ Am ⟶ D⁷ ⟶ G⁷ ⟶   C

'Ru - dolph, with your nose so bright, won't you guide my sleigh to - night?' ___ Then how the rein - deer

Secondary 7ths are frequently used in inversion, as in the next example (in which the progression of secondary 7ths is shown in small notes below the main stave):

Mozart: Piano Sonata in G, K 283

Ex. 3.18.5

E⁷ ⟶ A⁷ ⟶ D⁷ ⟶ G⁷ ⟶ C

Look again at Examples 3.18.4 and 3.18.5 on the previous page and see if you can spot an old friend. It is the circle of 5ths, but with more major chords than before: E^7–A^7(or Am)–D^7–G^7–C. As these two examples show, the falling-5ths progression can be found in music of very different times and styles.

A note about accidentals

Because secondary dominants are chromatic they always involve the use of accidentals, and so this is a good moment to review the various different purposes for which accidentals are needed. They may be

✦ The raised or lowered versions of notes 6 and 7 in a minor key

✦ Chromatic alterations, such as those needed in secondary dominant chords

✦ Pitches needed for a new key because of a modulation.

In other words, an accidental doesn't always mean a modulation! In fact, modulation from a minor key to its relative major can even occur without any accidental at all, as it is often possible just to stop sharpening the minor key's leading note – as when C♯ becomes plain C in bars 2 and 3 of Example 4.4 on page 53. Remember, it is the presence of a definitive cadence that really confirms the key of the music.

Activity 3.18

(a) Identify two secondary dominant chords in the following passage and describe the function of each (e.g. V^7 of iii).

James Molloy: *Love's Old Sweet Song*

(b) Name the final cadence in this extract.

(c) Does the music *above* modulate?

(d) Name the harmonic progression used in bars 5–8 of the passage.

(e) Change the chords marked * *below* into secondary dominants by adding the appropriate accidentals.

3.19 The tierce de Picardie

Play the following passage:

Ex 3.19

Mundy: *Ah, Helpless Wretch*

G minor   V ⟶ I♮3

Although the key is G minor, the final tonic chord is G *major*. When a major version of chord I is used to brighten the ending of a passage in a minor key it is known as a **tierce de Picardie**. The origin of the term is unclear, but 'tierce' refers to the 3rd of the tonic chord (which is unexpectedly major) and it seems likely that this practice was associated in bygone times with music from the region of Picardy in France.

Example 3.19 was composed in about 1585, at a time when composers were reluctant to end significant sections of a piece on a minor chord. Instead, 16th- and 17th-century composers usually preferred to end a minor-key passage with bare octaves or a bare 5th (as in the last example on the previous page) – or else they would use a tierce de Picardie in order to end on a major chord.

The tierce de Picardie thus occurs as the final chord of perfect and plagal cadences in many renaissance and early baroque pieces and is not regarded as a type of modulation. By the late-18th century the use of this device had become rare, as composers increasingly accepted the slightly sour effect of actually ending on a minor chord.

Activity 3.19

Name the key of each of the following passages, label the chords and then add an accidental to create a tierce de Picardie at the end of each.

3.20 Harmonic rhythm

As you worked through the music in this chapter you may have noticed that in the more hymn-like examples (such as those above) the chords change on almost every note, while in others (such as the song in Activity **3.18** (a) *opposite*), the chords change once a bar or less.

The rate at which chords change is known as the **harmonic rhythm** and is an important element in the style of different types of music. It is a subject that we will return to in some of the chapters in part II of this book.

4 Part-writing and non-chord notes

4.1 Definition of part-writing

Part-writing concerns the correct and stylish movement of individual parts within the chosen harmonies. In other words, part-writing is not about how you choose chords, but how you make best use of them when writing parts for instruments or voices. 'Voice-leading' is an alternative term for part-writing.

4.2 Tips for effective part-writing

Example 4.2.1 shows the progression vi–ii–V in C major. If this was allocated to three voices or instruments as it stands, the three parts would jump around in a disjointed way and would have no independence because they all move in **similar motion**, as shown by the staves on the *right*:

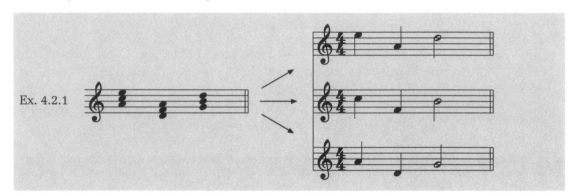

Compare this with the layout of the same three chords shown in Example 4.2.2 *below*. While the lowest of the three parts (the 'bass' of the harmony) still contains leaps, the two upper parts move much more smoothly because they use either stepwise movement or melodic intervals no larger than a 3rd.

Also, the highest part gains independence from the bass by moving in **contrary motion** – when the bass goes down, it goes up, and *vice versa*. All of this has been achieved simply by using an open spacing for the second of the three chords.

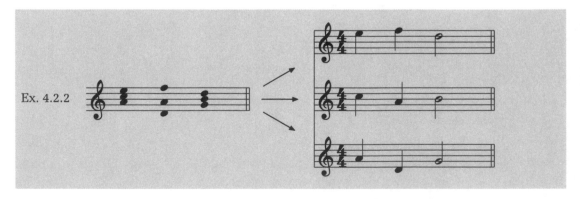

One of the secrets of good part-writing is to avoid large leaps, especially in the upper parts. You can avoid them by **adjusting chord spacing and note-doubling** – and perhaps by choosing an inverted chord rather than one in root position – in order to maximise the amount of stepwise (**conjunct**) movement.

It is not always possible to avoid large leaps in a melody or bass, but it is often best if the note after such a leap returns within the span of the interval:

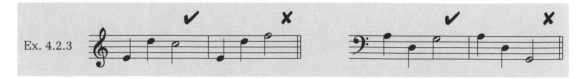

Ex. 4.2.3

When laying out parts, remember the following points:

✦ Large leaps occasionally occur in melodies (and frequently in bass parts) but it is best to return within the interval whenever possible, as shown *above*.

✦ It is often good for inner parts to move as little as possible – frequently staying on the same note works well. Otherwise try to keep to conjunct movement and small leaps (especially 3rds).

✦ The frequent use of contrary motion between the melody and bass will help give these two most important parts a real sense of independent movement.

✦ A good texture can be achieved by keeping the upper parts fairly close together – in contrast, a sizeable gap (even of an octave or more) between the bass and the next part up will help give focus to the bass, and prevent it being muddied by other parts close by.

Names of voice parts

Four-part writing is often for voices, and the parts are named after the voices that sing them. The two-stave layout of Example 4.2.4 *below* is typical. The topmost part is the **soprano**, written with upward stems. The part with downward stems on the same stave is the **alto**. The part with upward stems on the second of the two staves is the **tenor**, and the part with downward stems on this stave is the **bass**.

Example 4.2.4 shows a passage of simple yet effective four-part writing. The middle parts, while straightforward, have some melodic character and are never awkward to sing. All but one of the chords is in root position, so there are inevitably some leaps in the bass, although never more than a perfect 5th in this example.

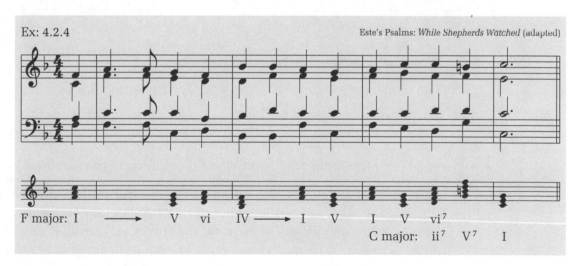

Ex: 4.2.4

Este's Psalms: *While Shepherds Watched* (adapted)

F major: I ⟶ V vi IV ⟶ I V I V vi⁷

C major: ii⁷ V⁷ I

The chords that form the basis of this passage are shown on the small stave at the bottom of this example. Carefully study the way in which they have been used to create upper parts that avoid jagged contours.

Every triad has a doubled root in the four-part version and the 5th is omitted in the final chord, resulting in the root (C) appearing in three of the four parts. The use of a first-inversion chord of C major (three chords before the end) helps to prevent too many leaps in the bass. The 5th has been omitted from chord ii^7 (and the root of this chord is doubled) again to maximise the amount of conjunct movement.

Complete the missing alto and tenor parts in the following progressions, using the chords indicated.

In (i) keep the alto on the same note throughout and make sure that the tenor moves entirely by step.

In (ii) the alto should either stay on the same note or move by no more than a semitone, and the tenor should not leap by more than a 3rd.

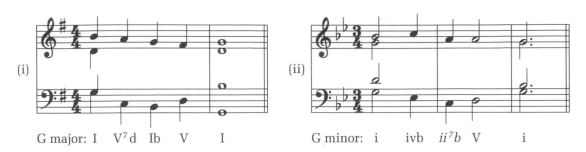

(i) G major: I   V⁷d   Ib   V   I

(ii) G minor: i   ivb   *ii⁷b*   V   i

A useful tip

When starting out on exercises of this sort, many people find it helpful to write down the notes of the chords in root position on a mini-stave, as shown *below*. Make sure you take account of sharps or flats in the key signature and in minor keys be certain to include the necessary accidental for the raised leading-note.

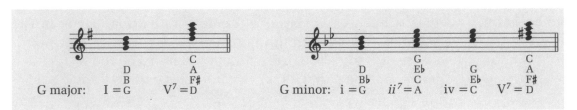

You should make similar mini-staves for yourself when working on later exercises, until you really feel confident in knowing the chords for the key concerned.

4.3 Parallel perfect 5ths and octaves

Ex. 4.3.1

G: I   V

The person who wrote Example 4.3.1 has done two things which are unwise:

✦ Doubling the 5th in chord V without any good reason (normally the root should be doubled whenever possible)

✦ Letting the tenor leap a 4th when it could have repeated the D in the first chord.

As a result the tenor and bass move in **parallel perfect 5ths**, often referred to as **consecutive 5ths**. In traditional harmony there is a ban on parallel perfect 5ths in the same pair of parts, as well as on **parallel octaves** and **parallel unisons**. This is because these particular consecutive intervals rob the parts involved of their individuality.

You need to be aware that there has to be some movement before consecutives are caused – simply repeating a 5th, as in Example 4.3.2, is fine.

Ex. 4.3.2

F: I   I

You should also realise that we are referring only to the basic parts in traditional harmony. It is common to double a melody or bass in octaves for a complete phrase (or longer) in many other types of music (as in the piano extract printed *opposite*). And in less traditional harmony, composers such as Debussy have made effective use of sonorities produced by parts moving in consecutive 5ths. But for the purpose of harmony exercises, consecutive 5ths, octaves and unisons must be avoided.

When checking for forbidden consecutives, you need to examine every combination of two parts. In four-part writing that means six checks:

✦ Soprano and alto
✦ Soprano and tenor
✦ Soprano and bass
✦ Alto and tenor
✦ Alto and bass
✦ Tenor and bass.

In the following example there are consecutive octaves between soprano and bass, and alto and bass, plus three sets of consecutive 5ths between other pairs of parts:

Ex: 4.3.3

Activity 4.3

Indicate consecutive 5ths and consecutive octaves in the following passages by drawing arrows between the notes concerned (as in Example 4.3.3 *above*). There are three forbidden consecutives in the first example and four in the second.

(i)

(ii)

4.4 Other types of movement

Occasional parallel 3rds or 6ths can be effective, but parallel 2nds and 7ths are not part of traditional harmonic styles. As we saw on page 50, contrary motion is preferable between soprano and bass, and makes it much easier to avoid forbidden consecutives between these parts. In the following example notice how Schumann's strong bass part in octaves moves mainly in contrary motion to the melody.

Ex: 4.4   Schumann: *Album for the Young*, No 41

Oblique motion, in which one part stays on the same pitch while the other part moves up or down, is another good way of achieving independent soprano and bass parts, and of avoiding consecutives. An example of oblique motion is shown near the start of the music for Activity **4.4** *below*.

Activity 4.4

Between the staves in the following music, write '**C**' where there is contrary motion, '**S**' for similar motion, and '**O**' for oblique motion. The first answer is given.

Sibelius: *Finlandia* (adapted)

4.5 Tendency notes

Good part-writing involves controlling the various parts, but the best results come when we work *with* the notes rather than trying to force them artificially.

In section **3.2** (on page 33) we noted that the leading note (note 7 of the scale) has a strong tendency to rise to the tonic. Other notes also have strong tendencies to move in certain directions – particularly notes that do not belong to the chord currently in use and the dissonant 7th in seventh chords. We shall find out more about these now.

4.6 An introduction to non-chord notes and dissonance

To make music more interesting, composers often include notes that are not part of the current chord. For example, we might briefly hear a D in one part while other parts are sounding a C-major chord. These additional notes help to provide rhythmic movement and a better sense of melodic flow, and may be termed **non-chord notes**. Some people call them **unessential notes** because they are not essential to the basic harmony, but this risks undervaluing the vital effect they have.

To see how important non-chord notes are to so much music, play the whole of the following example. Version (i) shows the chords in a two-part layout. Version (ii) fills many of the gaps between notes in the melody of the first version, showing how the basic harmonies support a well-known tune:

Ex: 4.6 (i)

Ex: 4.6 (ii)

Traditional (arranged Grainger): *Country Gardens* (adapted)

4.7 Passing notes

The most common type of non-chord note is the **passing note**. Where there is a leap of a 3rd a passing note can be inserted to fill in the gap with stepwise movement and so add rhythmic life and movement. Never forget: **a passing note must always be approached and quitted by step in the same direction**, which can be up or down.

Unaccented passing notes

Ex. 4.7.1

C: iii   vi

Look back to Example 4.6 (ii) on the previous page. The semiquavers are all passing notes. To be more precise, they are all **unaccented passing notes** – that is, they don't come on the beat, they just fill the gaps between chord notes. Most passing notes are unaccented and half a beat in length, like the one marked ∗ in Example 4.7.1 – those in Example 4.6 are only semiquavers because the tune is particularly jaunty.

Here are some more points about unaccented passing notes. Letters in brackets refer to the illustrations in Example 4.7.2 *below*.

✦ A passing note may lie between two notes from the same chord (a), or two notes belonging to different chords (b).

✦ Two passing notes may be used at the same time, making parallel 3rds (c) or, less often, parallel 6ths. Or they may move in contrary motion, usually with a 10th moving to a 6th via an octave or *vice versa*, as shown in (d). Very occasionally three passing notes are used at once.

✦ **Passing notes can cause consecutives** (e) where there would not have been any before (f).

✦ Passing notes may occur in any part, but too many can sound fussy.

✦ Passing notes are usually **diatonic** (that is, they use notes from the current key, like those *below*), although chromatic passing notes are possible.

Ex: 4.7.2   (a)   (b)   (c)   (d)   (e)   (f)

Accented passing notes

Accented passing notes come *on* the beat, and are therefore rhythmically stronger than the harmony notes on either side. Like the unaccented type, they fill the gap between two harmony notes and provide additional rhythmic interest, but we hear more clearly the harmonic conflict between the non-chord note that creates the accented passing note and the underlying chord.

This conflict is known as **dissonance** and, used in a controlled way through stepwise movement, can spice-up music, rather like adding pepper to make a meal more tasty. The chord progression in Example 4.7.3 (a) is repeated at (b) with accented passing notes in the melody. They are printed more lightly to reveal the underlying chords.

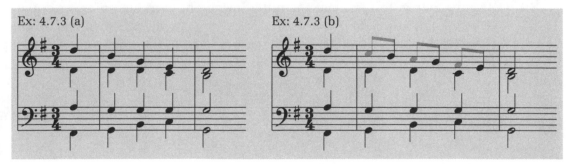

Ex: 4.7.3 (a)   Ex: 4.7.3 (b)

(a) Write 'PN' over each (unaccented) passing note in the melody of the following dance, and 'APN' above each accented passing note.

Haydn: Minuet, Hob IX:3, no 12 (adapted)

When you have finished, check that all remaining unmarked notes in the melody are harmony notes that belongs to the current chord.

(b) Add unaccented passing notes to *both parts* in the following passage to provide additional semiquaver movement. The key is E minor and so, if you choose to add passing notes at any of the places marked * you will have to consider whether it is better to use the normal version of note 6 (C) or the raised version (C♯).

Senaillé: Sonata in E minor (adapted)

A suggestion for the first complete bar is printed on the small stave above the music, but you don't have to follow this unless you wish. Be careful not to overload the piece with passing notes – it is not necessary to add them in every place where they might be possible.

4.8 Auxiliary notes

An **auxiliary note** lies a semitone or tone above or below two harmony notes **of the same pitch**. Auxiliary notes work in the same way as passing notes, except that they return to their starting pitch instead of carrying on up or down the scale. Example 4.8.1 includes three auxiliary notes, marked *. Notice that all three are diatonic and are short in relation to the harmony notes preceding and following them.

Ex. 4.8.1

Scottish traditional melody:
The Skye Boat Song

The chromatic auxiliary notes (marked * below) in Sousa's march 'The Liberty Bell' are an important feature of the piece. Play the following extract, and then see how ordinary the music sounds if you substitute G♮ for G♯ in bar 1 and F♮ for F♯ in bar 5.

Ex. 4.8.2

Sousa: *The Liberty Bell*

Activity 4.8

(a) Label each auxiliary note 'Aux' and each passing note 'PN' in the piece *below*.

(b) Write **X** beneath a secondary dominant chord and **Y** beneath a cadential $\frac{6}{4}$.

Gruber (melody): *Silent Night*

4.9 Suspensions

People sometimes find suspensions quite difficult to understand. First, here is an explanation with a minimum of jargon. A **suspension** happens

✦ At a change of chord, when
✦ One part hangs on to a note from the old chord, creating a clash, after which
✦ The delayed part falls by step to a note of the new chord.

Example 4.9.1 (a) shows four chords in G major and (b) shows the same progression with a suspension in the tenor part, marked with an arrow. When soprano, alto and bass move to chord V on the last beat, the tenor is left behind. Its G is not part of the D-major chord. The resulting clash is resolved when the tenor catches up by falling to F♯, a note that *is* part of the new chord of D major.

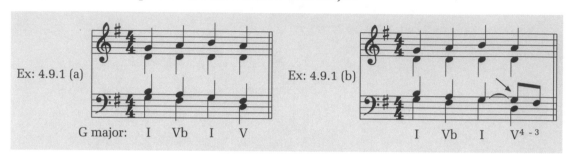

Ex: 4.9.1 (a) G major: I Vb I V

Ex: 4.9.1 (b) I Vb I V⁴⁻³

The suspended note in this example is shown tied to the previous note, but it could have been re-sounded, as shown in Example 4.9.2 (a), or written as a dotted note, as shown in Example 4.9.2 (b) *below*. These are both suspensions.

Ex. 4.9.2 (a)　Ex. 4.9.2 (b)　Ex. 4.9.2 (c)

Note that **not every tied note is a suspension**. There is no suspension in Example 4.9.2 (c) *above*: the D in the alto remains a chord note, and so we hear no clash.

Here now is a second description of a suspension, which will introduce you to the necessary technical vocabulary. A suspension happens in three stages:

✦ The **preparation**: the note that will cause the suspension is first heard as part of a normal chord, usually on a rhythmically weak beat.

✦ The **suspension** itself: the prepared note is held over (or repeated) as the other parts move to a different chord on a stronger beat, creating a dissonance between the bass and the suspended note.

✦ The **resolution**: on a rhythmically weaker beat, the suspended note falls by step to a note of the new chord in order to 'resolve' the dissonance.

Look again at the suspension marked by an arrow in Example 4.9.2 (a). By staying on G the tenor has temporarily replaced the 3rd of the D-major chord – this 3rd only appears when G resolves to F♯. Most suspensions follow this pattern. The suspension temporarily replaces the 3rd or root of the chord with a note that is one step higher. The suspended note then falls by step to the expected note, as seen here.

In most cases, **the resolution should not be sounded in any other part**, since this can create a very harsh dissonance, although we shall note an exception to this later. Suspensions can occur in any part, although they are least common in the bass.

Suspensions are classified according to the intervals between the suspended part and the bass at the moments of suspension and resolution. Three intervals are dissonant with the bass – 4ths, 7ths and 9ths. These give us the three main types of suspension:

✦ **4–3**, in which the 3rd of a root-position chord is temporarily replaced by a 4th above the bass. This then drops to the 3rd, as in Example 4.9.3 (a) *below*.

✦ **7–6**, in which the root of a first-inversion chord is temporarily replaced by a 7th above the bass. This then drops to a 6th above the bass, as in Example 4.9.3 (b).

✦ **9–8**, in which the upper root of a root-position chord is temporarily replaced by a 9th above the root in the bass. This 9th then drops a note to the upper root, as in Example 4.9.3 (c). This is the one type of suspension in which the resolution will already be sounding, since the root occurs in both the bass part and the resolution.

In all three cases, remember that the intervals can be compound. For instance, a 4th includes a compound 4th (that is, an octave plus a 4th).

Suspensions appear in many types of music, especially that of the baroque period. Often in renaissance and baroque music dissonances underline words that express pain or sorrow, but more often they simply provide valuable additional rhythmic movement. They are also useful in creating pleasing contrasts between tension (dissonance) and release (resolution) in the music.

Example 4.9.4 is from a trio sonata by Corelli. The suspensions (indicated by arrows) come in quick succession, the resolution of one serving also as the preparation of the next. This produces a **chain of suspensions**.

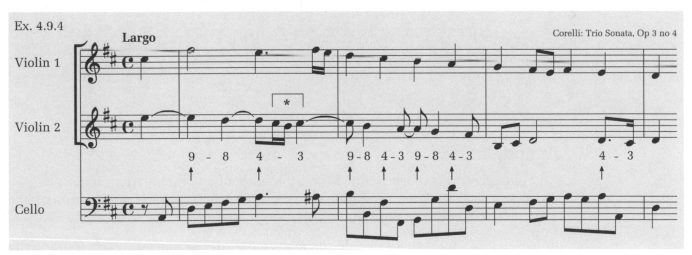

In this example, notice how:

✦ The dissonance sounds for only a quaver in most of the suspensions – but the first one lasts for a crotchet. To maintain rhythmic interest, Corelli makes the bass part start moving (with a passing note on E) before the suspension has resolved.

✦ One resolution (marked ⌐ * ⌐ *above*) is decorated with a lower auxiliary – a very common baroque technique. While D and C♯ crotchets would have been perfectly satisfactory, the semiquaver 'twiddle' adds interest in this slow-moving texture.

Another way to decorate a resolution is to leap to a different chord note between the suspension and its resolution, as shown by the note marked * in Example 4.9.5.

The music *below* shows the parts for two violins and cello in another trio sonata by Corelli. Notice that the second violin part on the middle stave is sometimes higher than the first violin part on the top stave. These are therefore called **crossing parts**.

(a) Identify each suspension in this passage by writing the letters **P** above the preparation, **S** above the suspended note and **R** above the resolution. Also show the type of suspension by writing 4–3, 7–6 or 9–8 below the suspended note and its resolution. The first answer has been done for you.

(b) Write ⌐ * ⌐ above a suspension in this passage that has a decorated resolution, and draw a circle around a tie that does **not** involve a suspension.

(c) Add the indicated suspensions to the passages below by completing the soprano part in (i) and the alto part in (ii). Each needs three crotchets – one for the preparation, one for the suspension and one for the resolution.

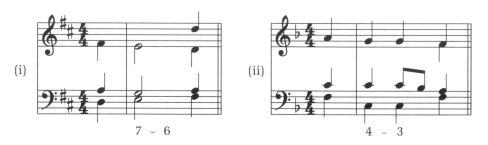

4.10 Appoggiaturas

An **appoggiatura** is rather like a suspension without any preparation. It consists of a dissonance followed by a resolution on a weaker beat. The word appoggiatura means 'leaning note', describing the way the dissonance leans onto its resolution.

In bar 3 of the following example there are four pairs of quavers, each forming the type of 4–3, 6–7 or 9–8 pattern above the bass that we saw used in suspensions. But these dissonances are not prepared like suspensions, nor are they approached by step like accented passing notes. Each note marked * is an appoggiatura.

The 'leaning' effect of an appoggiatura is often used as an expressive device in songs – as at start of *Yesterday* by Lennon and McCartney or in this famous tune from the 1961 film, *Breakfast at Tiffany's*:

Ex. 4.10.2
Henry Mancini: *Moon River*

Moon Ri - ver, wi - der than a mile I'm cross-ing you in style some day.

Appoggiaturas sometimes resolve upwards, like the one marked * in the music for Activity **4.10** *below*. In fact, this is a **chromatic appoggiatura** because C♯ is not part of the key of C minor. Most chromatic appoggiaturas tend to resolve upwards.

In the 18th century, an appoggiatura would often be written as a small note, like an ornament, thus making the resolution (the actual harmony note) clearer:

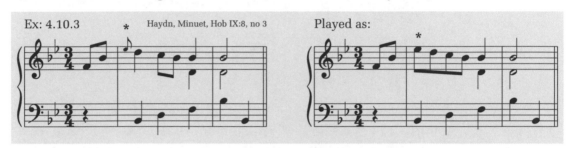

Ex: 4.10.3   Haydn, Minuet, Hob IX:8, no 3   Played as:

Activity 4.10

Write **X** above each diatonic appoggiatura in the following passage and * above each chromatic appoggiatura. The key is C minor and the first chromatic appoggiatura has been marked for you.

Mozart: Piano Sonata in C minor, K 457

4.11 Anticipations

Ex. 4.11

An **anticipation** is a weak-beat dissonance that does what it says – it anticipates the next harmony note by introducing it before the rest of the chord.

Anticipations are usually short and typically involve sounding note 1 in the melody immediately before chord I in a perfect cadence, as shown by the note marked * in Example 4.11.

4.12 Seventh chords: built-in dissonance

Revise sections **2.11–2.13** if you are unsure about using seventh chords.

The dissonances described so far all use notes foreign to the underlying harmony. For example, you can remove a passing note and the basic harmony will be unchanged, even though the music may sound less interesting. However, a dissonance (namely the 7th above the root) is an integral part of the harmony in seventh chords.

In traditional harmony, the 7th of a seventh chord, like all other dissonances, needs to be resolved. Example 4.12.1 *below* shows V^7 resolving to I in the key of D major, including various possible spacings and inversions.

The descending stepwise resolution of the dissonant note (the 7th above the root) is indicated by a *downward* arrow in each case. Chord V^7 also contains the leading note which, as you know, has a tendency to move up to the tonic. This is shown by an *upward* arrow in each progression.

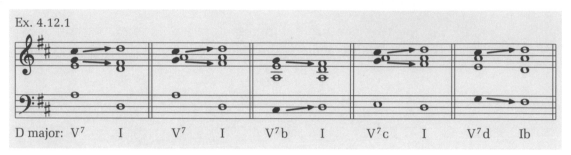

Ex. 4.12.1

D major: V^7 I V^7 I V^7b   I V^7c   I V^7d   Ib

The two tendency notes in V^7 pull in opposite directions – the 7th above the root wants to fall while the leading note wants to rise. This gives a powerful harmonic thrust from V^7 onto the following chord I – no wonder so many composers regularly prefer V^7 to V in perfect cadences!

Ex. 4.12.2

The 7th in chords such as ii^7 and the diminished 7th has a similar tendency to fall by step. And if you use chromatic notes, be aware that raised notes have a tendency to continue up a step while lowered notes want to fall a step. The chord marked * in Example 4.12.2 is a secondary dominant (V^7 of V). It contains a raised note that wants to move up and a 7th that wants to fall (both marked with arrows), rather like the two tendency notes in an ordinary dominant 7th chord.

Four final points:

✦ A tendency note should always be resolved in the **same** part.

✦ The dissonant note in a seventh chord is the **7th above the root** – this will not be a 7th above the bass note if the chord has been inverted.

✦ Because the 7th is in the bass in chord V^7d, its resolution must also be in the bass. If you use V^7d it is more or less inevitable that the next chord will be Ib, as seen in the last progression in Example 4.12.1.

✦ In the very common progression V^7–I, in which both chords are in root position, the resolution of the two tendency notes makes it impossible to include all notes of both chords when using four parts or fewer. You will need to omit the 5th (and instead double the root) in one or other of the two chords, as seen in the first two progressions shown in Example 4.12.1.

Activity 4.12

(a) Transpose Example 4.12.1 to the keys of G major, G minor, F major and C minor.

(b) How does chord V^7 in G major compare with chord V^7 in G minor?

5 Counterpoint

5.1 Introduction: what is counterpoint?

There is **counterpoint** when two or more parts have simultaneous melodies with clearly distinct rhythms. The listener is much more conscious of hearing different musical strands than in the kind of homophonic writing shown in Example 3.4.2 (on page 34) where the parts are identical in rhythm.

Here is an example of a **contrapuntal texture** ('contrapuntal' is the adjective which describes counterpoint):

Ex. 5.1   Bach: Two-part Invention, No 13

Counterpoint may be a kind of opposite of homophony. But it is not useful to think of it as the opposite of harmony.

Our study of harmony began with what we might call the *vertical* (or simultaneous) aspects of music – the sounding together of different pitches to form harmonic intervals, triads and other chords. And our definition of counterpoint does stress what we might call the *horizontal* aspects of music. But harmony concerns progressions, and to achieve good part-writing the layout of chords in progressions requires attention to 'horizontal' considerations, such as when we prefer stepwise movement and small leaps in upper parts, include plenty of contrary motion with the bass, and avoid consecutives 5ths and octaves.

However, the various melodic ('horizontal') parts in contrapuntal writing do not just go their own ways without regard for the resulting ('vertical') harmony. Look at Example 5.1 again and see how it is based upon chords I and V^7 of A minor. Traditional counterpoint of this sort is based on the types of chords described in Chapter 2. Two-part serial counterpoint (to be discussed in Chapter 9) follows very different paths, but it requires equally careful thought about what happens vertically, as explained in Section **9.14** of that chapter.

5.2 Some principles of counterpoint

In successful contrapuntal writing

✦ The principles of part-writing referred to in Chapter 4 are perhaps even more important (if that's possible) than in homophonic textures.

✦ The various parts are genuinely independent in rhythm for most of the time. There may be moments when two or more parts move together (for example in parallel 3rds or 6ths), but these should be fairly few in your own exercises.

✦ Parts often take it in turns to have the shorter note values. For instance, in Example 5.1, the right-hand part has shorter note values than the left to begin with, but this is reversed later.

✦ Each part has genuine melodic interest.

5.3 Making melodies interesting

What give a melody musical interest? Here are five things that help.

✦ **Rhythmic variety and balance**

Few melodies are based for long on only one or two note values. However, placing very short and very long notes next to one another is rarely convincing. Sometimes shorter notes are used more frequently as a melody unfolds and as excitement grows (for example in the melody of Example 4.10.1 on page 60).

✦ **Balance between ascending and descending movement**

A large leap is often followed by movement in the opposite direction. In Example 5.3.1 each rising interval is followed by a mainly stepwise fall. The resulting succession of descending phrases combines with the minor key and slow speed to create the nostalgic character of this famous melody.

Ex. 5.3.1
Adagio
Albinoni (arr. Giazotto): *Adagio*

✦ **Balance between stepwise movement and leaps**

Melodies in most musical styles have a good deal of stepwise movement, but too much can be dull, and at least a few leaps are essential to give shape to a tune. For instance, see the melody of *Moon River* quoted in Exercise 4.10.2 on page 61, where the leaps occur at the *start* of each descending phrase, rather than *after* each phrase, as they do in Example 5.3.1 *above*.

Too many leaps may be distracting and restless in some styles, although plenty of large leaps (together with a restless effect) are more or less inevitable in serial music. Look again at Example 4.9.4 on page 59. Corelli's violin parts could easily be sung, because they feature mainly stepwise movement, but his cello part contains numerous octave leaps and is much more instrumental in style.

✦ **Use of a reasonable range**

In conventional melody writing, too much emphasis on a small number of pitches can sound tedious – it is as though the tune doesn't seem to be getting anywhere. In many instrumental melodies the composer deliberately exploits the player's ability to cover a considerable range of notes, and may therefore use much wider intervals than singers could manage.

Details about the ranges of various instruments are given on page 176.

This means knowing the range of the instruments for which you write, and also understanding a little about the different parts of that range. For example, although the flute can go as low as middle C, the bottom notes are quiet and easily masked by other instruments. In contrast, it can produce a clear, bright tone in its upper register, starting from D, a 9th above middle C, and continuing well into the leger lines above the treble stave. Flute parts generally sound better if kept fairly high.

✦ **Satisfying structure**

Composers give much thought to structuring their melodies. Repetition of a good idea makes a tune memorable, but exact repetition risks sounding boring and is often avoided. At bar 5 of *Moon River* (page 61), Mancini doesn't do the obvious and repeat all of the first four bars. Instead he starts with a repetition of bars 3–4 only, and then adds a new ending to complete his second four-bar phrase.

The melody in Example 5.3.1 *opposite* uses **varied repetition** in a different way. The second phrase (bars 3–4) is the same as the first, except that it is one step higher. This is known as a melodic **sequence** and it has the side effect of making the first phrase end on the leading-note (F♯) and the second phrase 'answer' it by ending on the tonic (G), thus satisfying the tendency of the leading note to rise to the tonic, although only after a tantalising gap in this example.

Too many sequences can sound as predictable as straight repetition, so the third phrase is considerably varied, but the basic scalic descent of the opening idea is still present in the notes G–F–E♭–D, despite the decoration with other pitches.

The overall shape of a melody is also important. We have already noticed that Example 5.3.1 consists of a succession of descending phrases. More optimistic melodies will often use ascending phrases. 'Arch' shapes are also widely used. In these the highest note may come near the start (as in *Moon River*), in the middle or near (but not at) the end.

Phrase construction

Play or sing the following well-known melody. It has four phrases of equal length, each with the same rhythm (slightly varied at the end of the third phrase).

Ex. 5.3.2

Hill: *Happy Birthday to You!*

- ✦ The first phrase establishes the rhythmic pattern of the song and rises to end on the leading note of F major.

- ✦ The second phrase is almost the same as the first, but at the end it rises one step higher, giving the sense that the tune is moving forward. By ending on the tonic it provides an answer to the first phrase and resolves its leading note.

- ✦ The third phrase uses the rhythm of the first two phrases (slightly varied at the end). It uses the same first two pitches, but after these it immediately leaps to a climactic top note, balanced by a descent in the rest of the phrase.

- ✦ The fourth phrase also uses the rhythm of the first two phrases. Again it begins with a pair of quavers of identical pitch, but this concluding phrase starts high and then descends to end on the tonic.

Activity 5.3

Using the above commentary as a model, describe how each of the following tunes is constructed. Identify climactic points and mention examples of varied repetition.

Arlen: *Somewhere Over the Rainbow*

Bach / Petzold (attrib.): Minuet in G

Brahms: *Cradle Song*

5.4 Imitation

If you have ever sung rounds such as *Three Blind Mice* or *London's Burning*, you will have heard **imitation**. It occurs when a melodic idea in one part is immediately taken up by another, while the first part continues. In the following round, first published in 1609, the second and third voices imitate the first part.

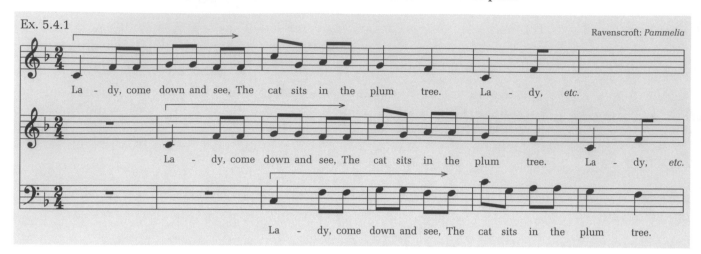

Ex. 5.4.1

Ravenscroft: *Pammelia*

La - dy, come down and see, The cat sits in the plum tree. La - dy, *etc.*

La - dy, come down and see, The cat sits in the plum tree. La - dy, *etc.*

La - dy, come down and see, The cat sits in the plum tree.

Imitation is often used in contrapuntal textures, although sometimes only for a few notes at a time. Look back to Example 5.1 on page 63 and notice how the left hand twice imitates the semiquaver patterns previously heard in the right hand.

In Example 5.4.1 *above*, the second voices enters at the same pitch as the first, and the bass is also the same, except for being an octave lower.

This is not always the case. In Example 5.4.2 *below* the **imitative entry** in the second part is a 4th lower than the same tune in the upper part, while in Example 5.4.3 the lower part enters first, and then the upper part imitates it a 5th higher. We could think of these as tonic- and dominant-based entries, and they are at least as common as imitation at the unison or octave.

Ex. 5.4.2

Bach: Fugue in C, BWV 846

Ex. 5.4.3

Bach: Fugue in C, BWV 846

Notice that in Example 5.4.2, the imitative part enters after only two beats (known as close imitation) while in Example 5.4.3 the imitation occurs six beats later. But in both cases the imitation is **exact** – in other words, all the intervals of the melody are the same in the imitated version, despite the difference in pitch.

Imitation is not always exact. In Example 5.4.4 on the next page, there are several differences between the vocal melody and its imitation in the accompaniment.

Interval **A**, originally a minor 2nd, becomes a minor 3rd when imitated and the triadic shape **B** becomes a stepwise descent. But we still hear this as imitation because the pitch outline is similar enough and, most importantly, the rhythm remains the same.

Ex. 5.4.4

Bernstein: 'Somewhere' from *West Side Story*

There's a   time for us,   Some day a   time   for us,

The reason for inexact imitation may be, as in this example, that the composer wants certain harmonies more than he wants exact imitation. Whether exact or inexact, imitation must make sense with the harmonies in the other parts.

Another reason is to allow a tonic–dominant shape in one part to be answered by a dominant-tonic shape in another, without causing unwanted modulation. The melody at the start of Example 5.4.5 begins with a lower auxiliary spanning a tone between the notes G and F, and then leaps down a 5th from dominant to tonic. When this is imitated a 4th higher, the lower auxiliary spans only a semitone (between C and B) and the melody then leaps down a 4th from tonic to the dominant below:

Ex. 5.4.5

Bach: *Goldberg Variations*, No 6

This is known as a **tonal answer**, because the changes keep the music within the same key. If Bach had used a **real answer**, in which the imitation exactly copies the intervals of the subject, the music would have started heading towards F major, as shown *left*, which would have been an unlikely key for a first modulation.

Imitation is often described in terms of the intervals separating the original and imitating parts. For example, the imitation in Example 5.4.2 is at the 4th below, in Example 5.4.3 it is at the 5th above, and in Example 5.4.4 it is at the octave above.

Activity 5.4

Draw brackets under the lower part in this passage of 16th-century music to show how the upper part has been imitated. Identify the interval of imitation in all three cases, and state which imitation is exact and which is the least exact of the three.

Taverner: *Gaude plurimum* (text omitted)

5.5 Canon

In a **canon** exact imitation continues for a considerable time (perhaps throughout a whole section or piece). Canon is often considered a rather learned device, and it does require considerable skill, but most people know a few simple canons, such as *Three Blind Mice*, *London's Burning* or *Frère Jacques*. These are all a type of canon known as a round, because you can keep the canon going round indefinitely by returning to the beginning of the melody as soon as you reach the end.

Other types of canon don't keep repeating like rounds, and they may be combined with other non-imitative parts within the contrapuntal texture.

The right-hand part of Example 5.5 shows the beginning of a two-part canon. The left-hand part is clearly contrapuntal, but it does not take part in the canon. Instead it provides a **free part** that supports the canon and makes the harmonic structure clearer and the texture fuller.

Ex. 5.5

Bach: *Goldberg Variations*, No 6

Notice how the use of sequence as well as canon binds this passage together, and how Bach is able to cover a wide range by making his bass part surge upward in contrary motion to the canonic parts, which plummet down across two octaves.

But don't let this example depress you! Bach was the most skilful of composers at working contrapuntal textures into brilliant and attractive pieces, and he was at the height of his powers when this music was first published in 1741. No composer has achieved quite such a reputation for contrapuntal skill in the more than two-and-a-half centuries since then.

Imitative and canonic textures are found less often in the classical style of the late-18th century and in the romantic style of the 19th century, but canonic writing came back into favour in 20th-century serialism (see Section **9.19** in Chapter 9).

Finally, note that canon is described in the same way as imitation – by naming the interval between the parts ('at the 5th below', and so on). So we can say that Example 5.5 includes a canon at the 2nd above.

6 Chorales

A chorale is a type of hymn that was traditionally sung in the Lutheran (Protestant) churches of Germany. The harmonisations of these tunes by J S Bach (1685–1750) have long been regarded as excellent models of four-part chordal writing.

Bach's settings can be found in a book called *Bach, 371 Harmonized Chorales and 69 Chorale Melodies with Figured Bass* edited by Albert Riemenschneider (published by Schirmer). This widely-available collection is commonly known as *Riemenschneider*. In the following sections the letter *R* plus a number refers to a chorale in *Riemenschneider*.

6.1 Chorales in exams

Edexcel AS

For Edexcel AS Music there is a coursework option in which you have to harmonise the cadences, including approach chords, in an otherwise complete harmonisation of a chorale. The tests are not usually taken straight from *R*, but are similar in style.

We shall prepare you for this kind of work in sections **6.6–6.14**. If you are not entering for the Edexcel AS examination, you should still work through these sections, as learning how to harmonise cadences is an important first step towards the more ambitious work described in the next paragraph.

Edexcel A2 and other exams

The traditional type of chorale harmonisation test (as, for example, in Edexcel A2 Music) requires you to harmonise several *complete* phrases of a chorale melody. Normally the full harmony of the opening bars is given, to provide a starting point and a guide to the style required. We shall deal with the harmonisation of complete phrases in sections **6.16–6.19**.

If you are studying Bach chorales for an exam other than Edexcel AS or A2 Music, be sure to check the current requirements. Section **6.20** deals with adding three upper parts to a given bass, as required in some other types of chorale test.

6.2 Writing for four-part choir

When writing chorale harmonisations it is best to keep within the vocal ranges shown in Example 6.2. The soprano range is included here for reference, although in most types of exam this part will be given.

Bass parts occasionally go a note or two lower than shown here – for example, at the end of a phrase in order to reach a low dominant or tonic in a perfect cadence.

In the rest of this chapter, we often refer to the soprano, alto, tenor and bass parts as S, A, T and B for short.

Chorales are normally written in short score – that is, with S and A on a treble stave, and T and B on a bass stave. The tails for S and T always go up, and the tails for A and B always go down, as in Example 4.2.4 on page 51.

6.3. The chorale style

There are a number of important points to note about the style of Bach's chorales, each of which we will explore in more detail during the course of this chapter:

✦ Each phrase ends with a cadence, shown by a pause sign (𝄐) on the last chord of the cadence.

✦ The majority of cadences are perfect, with both V$^{(7)}$ and I in root position. Most of the rest are imperfect cadences often with the first chord inverted.

✦ Chords usually change on every beat until a cadence. One or both chords of the cadence itself may last for more than one beat, but this not always the case.

✦ The harmony makes much use of primary triads and their inversions, along with the types of cadence approach we have studied, such as falling-3rd or falling-5th progressions, or the cadential $^6_4$.

✦ Some phrases are likely to modulate to closely-related keys.

✦ In many chorales, non-chord notes keep up an almost continuous flow of quaver movement until each cadence. However, the final chord of a cadence is not usually decorated – there is normally a clean break before the next phrase begins.

Although this final point means that melodic decoration is an essential part of the style, it is important to remember that Bach's basic harmony is mainly simple and homophonic in style – contrapuntal devices such as imitation are not used in four-part chorale settings.

A few of Bach's chorale settings have a special chromatic intensity, often because of words that refer to suffering or death. However, these are exceptional and unlikely to appear in exams. Indeed, exam exercises do not as a rule provide any words, but are concerned just with musical content and style of Bach's more typical settings.

6.4 Spacing of chords

The first kind of spacing shown in Example 6.4.1 *below* sounds well when sung by a four-part choir. It has a larger interval between T and B than between any other two neighbouring parts, giving real focus to the all-important bass part, and is a type of spacing that is very common in Bach's work.

The second type of spacing shown in Example 6.4.1 has small intervals at the top and bottom of the texture, and a large gap in the middle. This rarely sounds good for voices and was little used by Bach.

Ex: 6.4.1

Try to avoid more than an octave between any two of the three upper parts, but remember that a much bigger gap between T and B is fine. Here is an important tip that will help you capture Bach's style in your own work:

✦ **Keep the tenor part high**.

Bach's tenor parts are frequently on leger lines well above middle C. In fact, one of the most common faults in chorale tests is writing tenor parts that are far too low.

It may help to think of spacing in terms of keyboard playing. Many four-part vocal chords are easier to play with three notes in the right hand and one note in the left than with two notes in each hand. For instance, the last four chords of Example 6.4.2 (i) could be played as shown in Example 6.4.2 (ii).

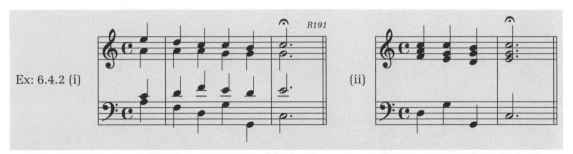

Activity 6.4

Here is a short passage designed for playing in the '3+1' manner shown in Example 6.4.2 (ii) *above*. Notice how little the top three parts move, and re-read what was said on pages 50–51 about aiming for stepwise movement in inner parts.

R303 (adapted)

6.5 Doubling

The three bullet points in section **2.16** (page 31) outlined how doubling works in triads and seventh chords. Here now is some more detail.

$\frac{5}{3}$ **chords**
✦ **Normally double the root.** You can instead have three roots and a 3rd, which means omitting the 5th, although Bach himself rarely does this.

✦ **Never omit the 3rd** – the result sounds bare and isn't clearly major or minor.

$\frac{6}{3}$ **chords**
✦ **Double any pitch that is note 1, 4 or 5 of the key you are in.** For example, if you use chord iib in the key of G major, double the note C, which is note 4 in the scale of G major. This method is easy to remember if you think of the notes to double (1, 4 or 5) as the 'primary notes' of the scale (like the primary triads, I, IV and V). It doesn't matter whether the doubled note is the root, 3rd or 5th of the chord.

✦ Alternatively, **double the root of the triad** (except in *viib*, because doubling the root in that chord would mean doubling the leading note). Other notes can be doubled instead, if this seems more sensible in context, but never double the leading note in any chord.

All chords
✦ **Don't double any of the tendency notes** (the leading note, 7ths, chromatic notes or dissonant notes). This is because any such doubling will result in consecutives when both tendency notes resolve in similar fashion. If you need to double a note in a seventh chord it is best to double the root and omit the 5th.

There are a couple of more advanced points about doubling later in this chapter, in Sections **6.8** and **6.11**.

(a) The following $\frac{5}{3}$ chords all lack an alto part, a tenor part or both. Add appropriate notes so that each has two roots, a 3rd and a 5th. Be careful, especially with (vi), that the chord spacing is suitable.

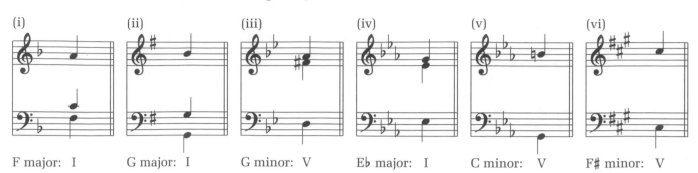

(i)	(ii)	(iii)	(iv)	(v)	(vi)
F major: I	G major: I	G minor: V	E♭ major: I	C minor: V	F♯ minor: V

(b) The following $\frac{6}{3}$ chords lack both middle parts. Add appropriate notes to complete each one, explaining which note you've doubled.

Write more than one completion if you can find two or more possible answers.

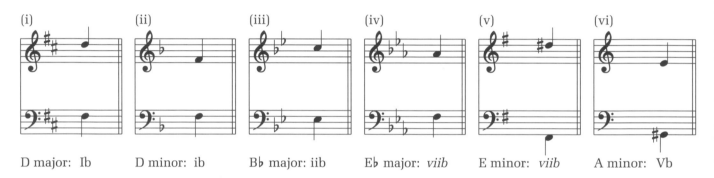

(i)	(ii)	(iii)	(iv)	(v)	(vi)
D major: Ib	D minor: ib	B♭ major: iib	E♭ major: *viib*	E minor: *viib*	A minor: Vb

6.6 Writing cadences

For the Edexcel AS Music exam you have to harmonise just the ends of phrases. This also makes a good starting point for other exams, since it is always best to begin with the cadences.

A phrase ending in exam tests usually consists of four chords, but for now we will concentrate on just the two final chords of a phrase. They most commonly form

✦ Either a **perfect cadence** (V–I)

✦ Or an **imperfect cadence**, ending on chord V (or occasionally Vb) and often with the first chord of the cadence inverted.

Plagal and interrupted cadences are little used in chorales. In fact, an interrupted cadence is never essential since a perfect cadence can always be used instead.

The type of cadence you write depends on the notes in the given melody. We will work largely in terms of common melodic patterns. A phrase that ends with notes 2 and 1, for example, is normally harmonised with a perfect cadence, because chord V will fit note 2 and chord I will fit note 1.

Matching scale degrees with chords in this way is very useful, but never forget that chorale harmonisation is not just 'composing by numbers'. Always hear and think about what you write.

When writing a cadence, follow these steps:

1   Identify the key at the end of the phrase

2   Identify the scale numbers of the final two notes (for example, 7–8)

3   Decide which type of cadence will best fit these notes, and write out the notes of the chords you will need

4   Work out what the bass notes are, and write them in

5   Add the alto and tenor parts

6   Check everything carefully, as explained on the next page.

6.7 Perfect cadences

Ex: 6.7.1

Example 6.7.1 shows a phrase from a chorale. Working through steps 1–3 *above* will tell you why this phrase must end with a **perfect cadence**.

1   The phrase ends in D major.

2   The two last notes of the phrase (E–D) are scale degrees 2–1.

3   The notes 2–1 will fit with a perfect cadence. Write down the notes needed for a perfect cadence in D major, perhaps on a mini-stave, as shown *left*.

4   Most perfect cadences in chorales are in root position, in which case the bass part should be A in chord V and D in chord I. A falling 5th from A to D works well, but a rising 4th provides desirable contrary motion between the outer parts:

Ex: 6.7.2

5   Now to add the inner parts – it is better to do this one chord at a time.

Chord V currently lacks its 3rd (C♯). This could be written a 3rd above the bass note but that would be far too low for a tenor part. Middle C♯ (an octave higher) would be fine for tenors, but that would leave no room for an alto note. The conclusion is inevitable: the altos must supply the C♯. That's all three notes of the triad accounted for, so the tenor must double a note, preferably the root (A).

Chord I currently has a doubled root (D), so the inner parts need to supply the 3rd (F♯) and preferably also the 5th (A):

Ex: 6.7.3

Did you spot the 'error' in the previous example? The leading note (C#) in the alto didn't rise to the tonic (D) in the way expected of a tendency note. In fact, this is not an error, but an important feature of Bach's chorale harmonisations:

✦ **If the leading note occurs in the alto or tenor at a perfect cadence, it often falls *directly* to the 5th of the tonic chord**.

Bach does this in order to achieve a complete and full-sounding tonic chord at the cadence, rather than the thinner sound of one without a 5th. You can see the difference by comparing versions (i) and (ii) in Example 6.7.4 *below*. Also, Bach occasionally allows a leading note in the tenor to leap upwards to the 3rd of the tonic chord at a cadence, again to achieve a complete tonic chord, as shown in (iv) *below*.

Such treatments of the leading note at cadences are a distinctive feature of Bach's chorales and you should try to use them whenever appropriate. But remember that the leading note should fall *directly* to the 5th of the tonic chord – Bach never uses a passing note between the two, as shown in Example 6.7.4 (iii). Be very careful about this, as spoiling a falling leading note by inserting a passing note to fill the gap is a common mistake in exams.

Ex: 6.7.4
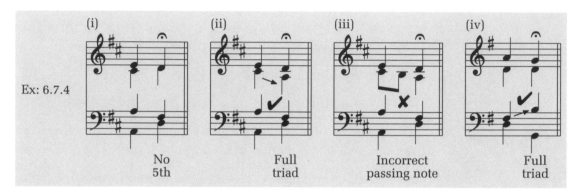

Before we move on to the final step in cadence writing, there is one improvement we can make to the cadence shown in (ii) *above*. In Section **6.3** we noted that

Ex: 6.7.5

Correct
passing note

✦ In many chorales, non-chord notes keep up an almost continuous flow of quaver movement until each cadence.

While a passing note in the alto would be incorrect, there is a better opportunity for a passing note in the tenor, between A and F#. This would introduce a G, forming a passing 7th above chord V that neatly resolves to F#. This is totally in keeping with Bach's methods and helps provide the really stylish result shown in Example 6.7.5.

All that remains is to complete the final stage in our six steps:

6   Check everything carefully on paper and by playing your work. Again, there are six stages in this process. Check that you have

✦ Used the right notes for the chords concerned

✦ Doubled (or omitted) notes correctly

✦ Spaced the notes so that there is no large gap between the three upper parts

✦ Used conjunct movement or only small leaps in the upper three parts

✦ Ensured that any tendency note in the first chord moves to the correct note in the second chord (remembering Bach's special treatment of the leading note when it occurs in an inner part of chord V at a perfect cadence)

✦ Avoided consecutive 5ths or consecutive octaves between any of the parts (as explained in Section **4.3** on pages 52–53).

If anything is wrong, correct it and then perform this six-point check again.

The tierce de Picardie was explained in Section **3.19** on page 49.

The fall from note 2 to note 1 in the soprano is the most common melodic pattern in perfect cadences. Here are four more examples from Bach's chorales – the perfect cadence in the last of these ends with a tierce de Picardie. The arrows in this example indicate leading notes that do *not* rise to the tonic.

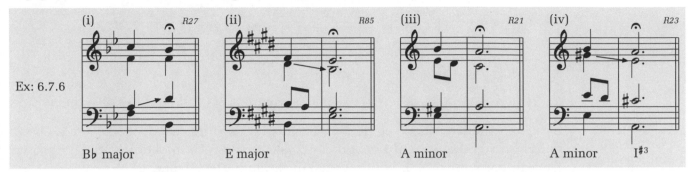

Ex: 6.7.6

Perfect cadences will also harmonise the melodic patterns 7–8, 2–3 and 5–3, as shown in Example 6.7.7. Cadence (iii) in this example shows the pattern 2–3 harmonised with an inverted perfect cadence (Vb–i). Inverted perfect cadences are much rarer than root position ones, and are never used at the end of a chorale.

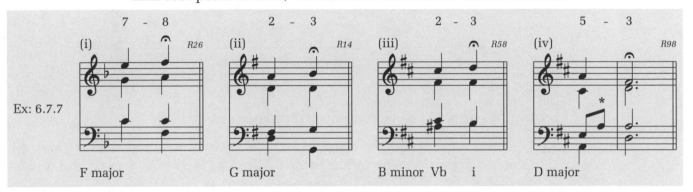

Ex: 6.7.7

Activity 6.7

(a) Which cadences in Example 6.7.6 at the top of this page include a dominant 7th as a passing note?

(b) Which of the following describes the note marked ✻ in cadence (iv) of Example 6.7.7 *above*?   auxiliary note   harmony note   passing note   appoggiatura

(c) Write a perfect cadence at the end of each of the following four chorale phrases. Follow the six steps outlined earlier, be sure to play your work, and remember to check it using the checklist printed *opposite*.

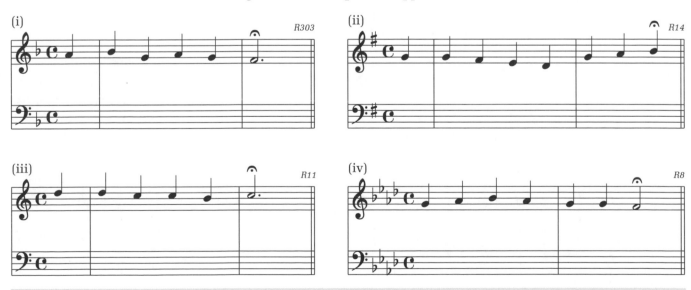

6.8 Imperfect cadences

Example 6.8.1 requires an **imperfect cadence**. If you follow steps 1–3 you'll see why.

Ex: 6.8.1

1   The key is A major.

2   The phrase ends with C#–B, which are notes 3–2 in the scale of A major.

In Bach's chorale harmonisations, roughly one in four cadences is imperfect.

3   The cadence cannot be perfect, because B does not occur in the tonic chord. However, there is a B in chord V (E, G#, B) and a C# in chord I (A, C#, E) so we can harmonise C#–B with I–V, making an **imperfect cadence**.

Ex: 6.8.2

                I   V

Look at this example as we continue with steps 4–6.

4   The bass must have A for chord I and E for chord V. It would be possible to fall from an upper A to the E, but rising a 5th from the lower A to the E provides desirable contrary motion between the outer parts.

5   Both chords are in root position, so double the root in each, and keep the inner parts as still as possible. The big gap (a compound 5th) between bass and tenor is perfectly acceptable.

6   As always, carefully check your work.

Doubling the major 3rd

Ex: 6.8.3

Ib   V

Bach often preferred to invert the first chord of an imperfect cadence, and Example 6.8.3 shows his own harmonisation of the cadence we have been working on, using the progression Ib–V. This results in a **doubled major 3rd** (C# in the outer parts) – Bach uses this pattern so often that it is well worth learning as an exception to the principles of doubling outlined on page 71. When he does so, note that (as here):

✦ Outer parts move in contrary motion, inner parts move as little as possible
✦ The bass includes a passing note between Ib and V.

Example 6.8.4 shows some more imperfect cadences in which notes 3–2 are harmonised with I–V or Ib–V. Note that Bach did *not* use Ic–V as an imperfect cadence in chorales. Ic–V is a typical formula for imperfect cadences in the classical style of the late-18th century (see Example 3.9.2 on page 39) but in chorales you should always find an alternative, as shown in cadence (iv) below.

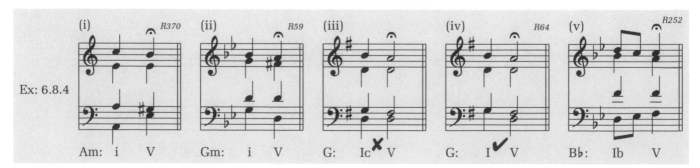

Ex: 6.8.4

  (i)   (ii)   (iii)   (iv)   (v)

Am: i   V   Gm: i   V   G: Ic ✗ V   G: I ✔ V   Bb: Ib   V

If the first chord of an imperfect cadence is not I or Ib, it will usually be a chord from the subdominant group – most often IV$^{(7)}$b or II$^{(7)}$b, as shown in Example 6.8.5. Notice how, in the first two of these cadences, Bach uses melodic decoration to maintain movement through the first (but not the second) chord of the cadence.

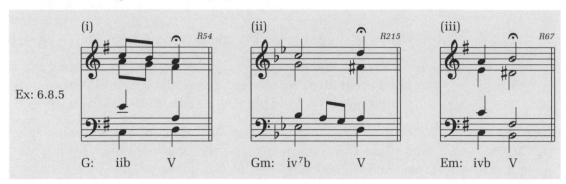

Ex: 6.8.5

Example (iii) *above* is a particular type of imperfect cadence known as a **phrygian cadence** – it consists of the progression ivb–V in a minor key, and is often used to harmonise notes 4–5 in minor-key cadences.

Activity 6.8

(a) Look again at cadence (i) in Example 6.8.4 *above* and then explain why Bach doubled the 5th of chord V instead of the root in this cadence.

(b) Why should notes 1–2 never be harmonised with chord IV–V? If this seems puzzling, try writing this progression in the key of C major, and note the problem it raises.

(c) Write an imperfect cadence at the end of each of the following three phrases.

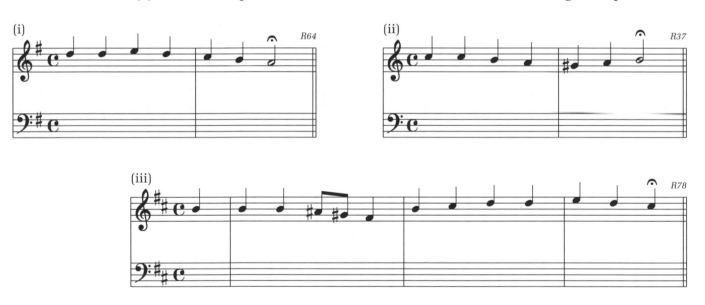

Ex: 6.8.6

Am: V^7 i

Sometimes the notes at the end of a phrase offer a choice of key and cadence. For example, phrase (i) in Activity **6.8** *could* end with a perfect cadence in A minor, as shown *left*.

When there is an alternative, the choice will depend on the context – what happens before and after the cadence, and whether modulation is desirable in the phrase concerned. In the middle of a chorale, Bach often preferred to modulate and use a perfect cadence in the new key, rather than an imperfect cadence in the tonic.

6.9 Choosing chords to approach a perfect cadence

First, a general point. It's best to change harmony on each crotchet beat (except on a long pause chord, which should have only one chord). In particular, don't repeat the same chord from a weak to a strong beat in your cadential progression – Bach only normally does this at the *start* of an anacrusic phrase, such as the opening of *R6* in Activity 6.17.2 on page 96). In common time (**C** or $\frac{4}{4}$), the weak beats are 2 and 4.

Here's how to choose the chord immediately before a perfect cadence in terms of some common melodic patterns. In all cases, the first and second notes are crotchets. The third note (the last of the phrase) may be a crotchet or longer.

Chord I as an approach

In the examples *below* the approach to chord V is often **directly from Ib, Ic or even from plain I**. Approaches from subdominant-group chords, common in much other music and illustrated in section **3.6** (pages 35–36), also occur – especially important are progressions including ii^{7}b, explained *opposite*.

Example 6.9.1 illustrates settings of some of the most common melodic patterns as well as some features of Bach chorales that should by now be becoming familiar:

✦ The first three cadences each include a passing 7th in the tenor, and most include at least one passing note

✦ Cadences (i), (iv) and (vii) have doubled major 3rds in chord Ib (as explained on page 76) with the characteristic passing note in the bass between Ib and V

✦ Cadences (ii), (iii) and (viii) include a falling leading-note in chord V

✦ Cadence (iii) includes a lower auxiliary in the bass (C) and finishes with a tierce de Picardie (as do perfect cadences at the *end* of most minor-key chorales).

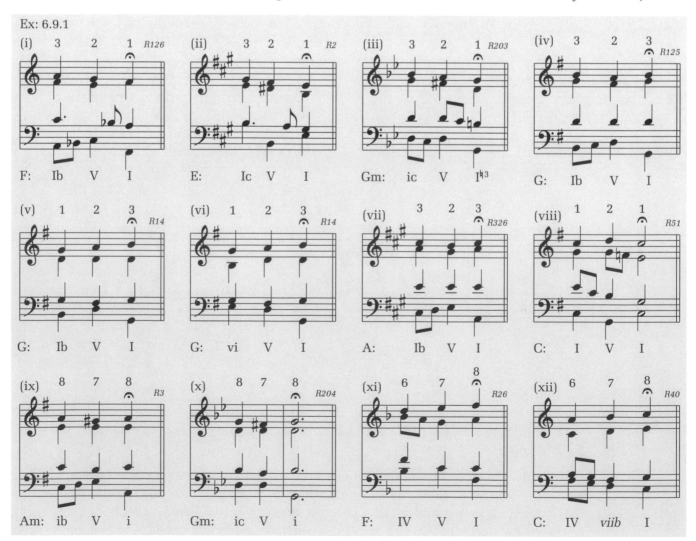

Cadence (xi) in the previous example harmonises the melodic pattern 6–7–8 with the progression IV–V–I. Although this seems temptingly obvious, it is potentially risky since the similar motion between S and B in chords IV–V can make consecutive 5ths or octaves in the middle parts difficult to avoid. In cadence (xii) Bach harmonises the same melodic pattern with IV–*viib*–I. Substituting *viib* for V allows contrary motion between the outer parts and reduces the risk of consecutives.

Chord ii⁷b as an approach

Sometimes the penultimate note of a phrase is a minim — usually as the middle note in the melodic pattern 3–2–1. The minim is often harmonised with *two* separate chords, resulting in a 'complete' four-chord cadence progression. (Exam questions on chorale cadences usually require you to write four chords at the end of each phrase.)

The following chord schemes for this pattern also work for the similar four-crotchet pattern 3–2–2–1 (just imagine the minim on pitch 2 split into two crotchets):

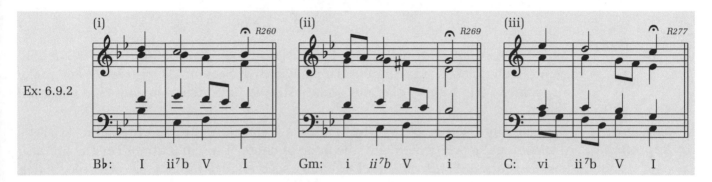

Ex: 6.9.2

All of these progressions use **II⁷b as the cadence approach chord**. And in every case the 7th of chord ii⁷b is treated as a suspension that resolves to the leading note – which in turn falls to the 5th of the tonic chord. Trace this pattern in the alto part of (i) and (ii), and in the tenor part of (iii).

This pattern also works well for melodies ending 8–8–7–8, in which the suspension can occur in the soprano part. In the following example, Bach approaches *ii⁷b* from chord VI – a falling 5ths pattern:

Ex: 6.9.3

Suspensions are also common in cases where Bach decides to harmonise a minim on pitch 2 with just a single chord V. Two full beats of 'plain' chord V would be very dull, so he uses a 4–3 suspension to keep up the musical interest. In Example 6.9.4 this occurs in the alto part in (i) and in the tenor in (ii). In both cases the pattern is similar to the suspensions in Example 6.9.2 *above* – the suspended note is the tonic and it resolves to the leading note, which then falls to the 5th of the tonic chord.

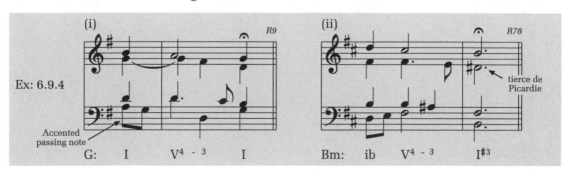

Ex: 6.9.4

Here are two more examples of ii⁷b used as a cadence approach chord, this time in the melodic pattern 4–3–2–2–1. In Example 6.9.5 (i) you could regard the second quaver beat as consisting of three simultaneous passing notes, but it actually creates chord Ic in passing, hence the expression 'passing $^6_4$'. Example 6.9.5 (ii) shows Ic more clearly used as a chord in its own right, although all the notes either move by step or stay put, so again it is really a passing $^6_4$.

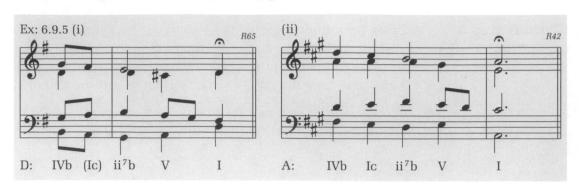

This progression, along with Ic–V–I, contains the only use of $^6_4$ chords commonly found in chorales. Read again the last paragraph of Section **2.4** on page 22 and **make a special note to be very cautious about using second-inversion chords in chorales.**

V⁷ of V as an approach

Occasionally Bach gives a perfect cadence a specially intense chromatic 'twist' by sharpening the 3rd (which is in the bass) of chord ii⁷b – in a minor key the 5th also has to be raised. This turns the chord into a secondary dominant – V⁷ of V (see section **3.18** on page 47 for more on secondary dominants).

Example 6.9.6 (i) shows V⁷ of V used to approach a perfect cadence in a major key – notice that this progression also includes another passing $^6_4$. V⁷ of V is more often used as an approach chord to perfect cadences in minor keys – an example is shown in (ii) *below*. If you decide to use this device, do so sparingly and remember to add the necessary accidentals (including any needed to cancel chromatic notes).

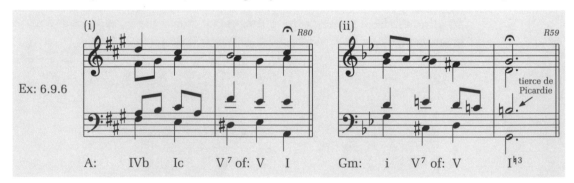

Activity 6.9

Add bass parts and chord symbols (but not inner parts) to complete the following progressions, which should each end with a perfect cadence.

Gm: G: F: Dm:

6.10 Choosing chords to approach an imperfect cadence

The most common type of imperfect cadence is I–V, and Bach generally approaches this from chord V$^{(7)}$b or its close relative, chord *viib*. Example 6.10.1 illustrates some of the possibilities.

The first three progressions are all from the same chorale and show how Bach sought to achieve variety, even when faced with similar cadences in the same key. All three patterns work equally well in major keys. Progression (iv) uses *vii^7* as an approach chord which, in a minor key as here, is a diminished 7th chord.

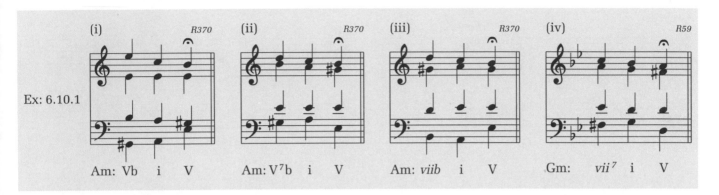

Ex: 6.10.1

Am: Vb i V   Am: V^{7}b i V   Am: *viib* i V   Gm: *vii^7* i V

Other approach chords include I, IV or VI – the choice depends on creating contrast with the first chord of the cadence as well as harmonising the given melody:

Ex: 6.10.2

Page 81
Exercise 6.10.2 (example iii) says that the second chord notated in the example is ii^{7}b. This is an error: the chord is actually ii^{7}c. In D minor, this is the supertonic chord in its second inversion form, ie an E minor chord with a B♭ bass note.

Sometimes the first note of an imperfect cadence is a minim, as shown in (i) *below*, or two crotchets of the same pitch, as shown in (ii).

In such cases it is not usually possible to use different chords for the two crotchet beats, as we did in the perfect cadence on the opposite page. However, as you can see in Example 6.10.3 *below*, Bach doesn't merely write a minim in all parts for chord I or repeat the chord exactly on the second crotchet beat – instead he maintains a sense of movement through the use of passing notes and/or additional harmony notes. Note especially how the octave leap in the bass of (i) *below* gives impetus to the second beat of the bar without actually changing the harmony.

The first of these progressions uses V^{7}b as an approach chord. The second has ivb.

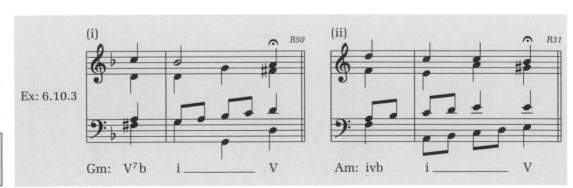

Ex: 6.10.3

Gm: V^{7}b   i _____ V   Am: ivb   i _____ V

(a) What type of melodic decoration is used in (i) the alto part and (ii) the tenor part of Example 6.10.2 (iii) on the previous page?

(b) What name is given to the particular type of imperfect cadence shown in Example 6.10.2 (iv) on the previous page?

(c) Add bass parts and chord symbols (but not inner parts) to complete the following progressions, which should each end with an imperfect cadence.

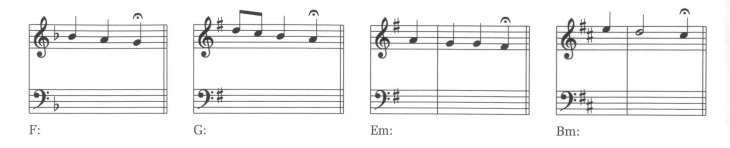

F: G: Em: Bm:

6.11 Part-writing in chorales

We covered the basics of part-writing in Chapter 4. This section rounds up a number of the more important points we encountered earlier and introduces some additional matters that are important in chorale settings. So far, most of the advice in this book has been positive, suggesting what you *can* do. But now we need to add a few points about what you should try *not* to do.

Crossing parts   Avoid crossing parts, such as letting the alto fall below the tenor, or the tenor below the bass. Although Bach occasionally does this, you will be well advised to avoid any part-crossing, unless you're absolutely certain that it is in Bach's style and makes the music better than it otherwise would be.

Overlaps   An overlap occurs if two neighbouring parts, such as tenor and bass, move so that the lower part in the second chord is higher than the upper part in the first chord, or *vice versa*, as shown in Example 6.11.1 (i) and (ii) *below*. This is best avoided by, for instance, choosing a different note to double.

Some overlaps are acceptable, such as the cadential progressions shown in (iii) and (iv) *below*, but even here the overlap could be avoided by taking the bass down to a low G.

Note that an overlap from the end of one phrase to the start of the next, as shown in (v), is perfectly acceptable. It may even be desirable when, as here, the new phrase doesn't start with a change of chord, and so needs a different layout of notes in order to sound distinct.

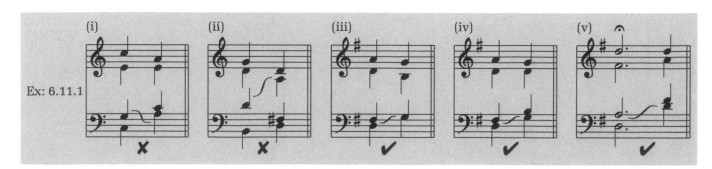

Ex: 6.11.1

Doubling

Revise the advice about doubling on page 71. Remember that

✦ Tendency notes, including the leading note and dissonances (2nds, 4ths or 7ths above the bass) must not be doubled

✦ Try to avoid doubling the 5th in root-position triads

✦ Bach sometimes doubles the 3rd in root-position and first-inversion chords but – and this is very important – he likes contrary motion and stepwise movement to and from the doubled 3rd

✦ Diminished triads (chord *vii*, plus chord *ii* in minor keys) are often used in first inversion with the bass note (the 3rd of the chord) doubled

✦ In chord Ic, the 5th should be doubled.

Dissonances

✦ The effect of a suspension or 7th chord is spoiled if the resolution of the dissonance is sounded at the same time in another part. The one exception is a 9–8 suspension, in which the note of resolution has to be in the bass below the suspended note.

✦ All suspensions, along with the 7th in chord ii^7(b) should always be prepared as well as resolved.

✦ When using the cadential $\frac{6}{4}$ (as in Ic–V–I), ensure that the 6th and 4th above the bass in chord Ic fall respectively to the 5th and 3rd above the bass in chord V. Bach regarded a 4th above the bass as a dissonance, so it should be prepared in the preceding chord whenever possible – failing that, it should be approached by stepwise movement from above.

✦ The 7th in chord V^7 can be treated a little more freely, but if it is not prepared then it should be approached by step.

Consecutives

✦ Consecutive 5ths, octaves or unisons between any pair of parts must be avoided.

✦ A perfect 5th followed by a diminished 5th in the same pair of parts is usually best avoided, especially between the bass and an upper part.

✦ A danger of too much similar motion between soprano and bass is the creation of **exposed 5ths** or **exposed octaves**. These can only occur between the outer parts, and only within a phrase (not between the end of one phrase and the start of the next). They happen where

   ✦ the soprano *leaps* and the bass moves in the same direction (by step or leap) so that the two parts arrive on a perfect 5th or an octave.

Exposed 5ths and octaves, shown in Example 6.11.2, sound poor because the perfect intervals concerned are too prominent – too 'exposed'.

✦ In the outer parts it is also preferable to avoid consecutive 5ths or octaves even when produced by contrary motion. These **5ths and octaves by contrary motion** are shown in (iii) and (iv) *below*.

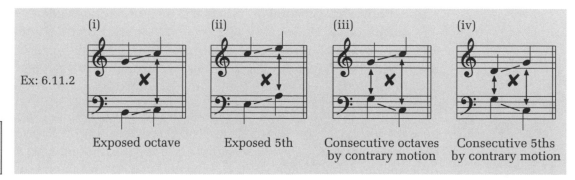

Ex: 6.11.2

(i) Exposed octave   (ii) Exposed 5th   (iii) Consecutive octaves by contrary motion   (iv) Consecutive 5ths by contrary motion

Because of these special points about the outer parts, never add A and T until you are sure there are no consecutive 5ths or octaves (including any by contrary motion) or exposed 5ths or octaves between S and B.

Then complete A and T, aiming for as much conjunct movement as possible, and finally carry out checks on all six pairs of parts, as shown at the top of page 53.

Sometimes it isn't easy to remove consecutives. If they exist between S and B before passing notes have been added, the choice of chords is faulty, so choose one or more different chords. If consecutives arise between other pairs of parts, the doubling in one or more chords may be unsuitable.

Too much similar motion between soprano and bass sometimes makes it difficult to avoid consecutives between other parts. They are far less likely to arise if **the bass moves in contrary motion to the soprano** as much as possible.

Activity 6.11

In the following two passages, someone who has not read section 6.11 carefully has made a number of mistakes, including awkward part-crossing, incorrect doubling, poor chord-spacing, overlapping and consecutives.

Find and label each mistake – the first one has been done for you.

Octaves by
contrary motion

6.12 Working a chorale cadences test

This section explains how to tackle the type of chorale cadences test set in Edexcel AS Music exams. However, it will be equally useful if you are taking a test in which you have to harmonise complete phrases from a chorale, since it is always best to begin with the cadences. We will look at harmonising complete phrases in Section **6.16** on page 91.

The method is simply an extension of the six steps listed at the top of page 73, but now we will be adding complete cadential progressions of three or four chords, rather than just a cadence, at the end of each phrase. Example 6.12.1 on the next page is a little shorter than an Edexcel test, but it will show you the steps to go through.

Ex: 6.12.1

1 **Identify the key at the end of each phrase**

The key of the first phrase is F major.
The second phrase begins by suggesting D minor but is in F major at the end.

2 **Work out the cadence and then the approach chords for the first phrase**

First identify the scale numbers of the last two notes of the first phrase. It ends A–G, which in the scale of F major is 3–2. We therefore choose an imperfect cadence, with final bass note C (for chord V). This C will lead on well to the bass C♯–D that follows the cadence. We can't be sure yet which bass note will precede the C, but pencil C into the bass part now and mark it V.

The most common approach to an imperfect cadence is from V$^{(7)}$b or *vii*b. Let's choose the latter (E, G, B♭ with G in the bass). This could lead neatly into Ib as the first chord of the imperfect cadence, so pencil in G and A into the bass at the start of the second complete bar and label G as *vii*b and A as Ib.

Now choose a chord for the end of the first complete bar. The quavers in the bass and tenor parts on beat 3 look very much like passing notes that are about to descend to F and A respectively. Combined with the given C in the melody, this would give chord I on beat 4. Pencil an F into the bass part and label it I.

3 **Work out the cadence and then the approach chords for the second phrase**

The second phrase ends G–F, which in the scale of F major is 2–1 and indicates a perfect cadence, with bass notes C–F. However, the penultimate melody note is a minim and so should preferably have two different chords, or at least a 4–3 suspension. Since the familiar progression ii^{7}b–V–I will fit this cadence, let's choose that. Pencil in the bass notes (B♭–C–F) and label the chords.

This just leaves the soprano A at the start of the cadential progression. Chord I would fit, but it seems a pity to anticipate the tonic chord at the end of the entire passage. Instead, let's take the opportunity to use chord vi, especially since this will give a highly desirable 'falling 5ths' progression from vi to chord ii in the next bar. Pencil in the bass note (D) and label it vi.

You should have the following skeleton harmonisation:

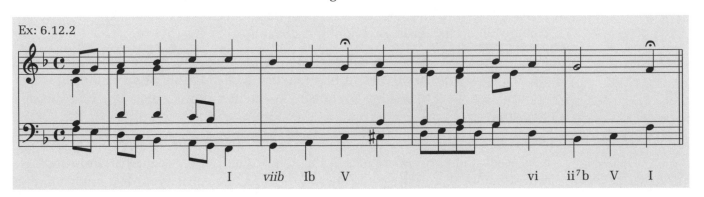

Ex: 6.12.2

I   *vii*b   Ib   V   vi   ii^{7}b   V   I

4   **Check the outer parts for consecutives**

Before adding the inner parts, check that there are no consecutives between S and B – don't forget that these can occur between the last printed notes of the phrase and your added parts, as well as within your own working. Here the risk of consecutives has been minimised by using mainly contrary motion in the bass.

5   **Add the alto and tenor parts**

Follow the usual methods for spacing and doubling. Remember to keep the tenor high and juggle the notes until you get as much conjunct movement as possible. Remember also to

◆   Look for clues at the end of the given part of a phrase. For example, at the end of the first complete bar the alto could stay on F, while the tenor B♭ is clearly a passing note which should lead to A in the last chord of the bar.

◆   Check that what you write for your first chord does not produce consecutives with the preceding given chord and that the chord on which you end a phrase doesn't produce consecutives with the given first chord of the next phrase.

◆   Make sure that if you use any chords that need special treatment, such as Ic or ii⁷b, then the discord is prepared, sounded and resolved in the same part. This is marked P, S and R in the example below.

By now, the working should look something like this:

Ex: 6.12.3

This is a good harmonisation, but it doesn't entirely capture Bach's style. For instance, it would be more convincing if the alto fell to C at the end to complete the final tonic chord and provide Bach's characteristic falling leading-note at a perfect cadence. But the main missing ingredient is the rhythmic flow produced by melodic decoration.

6   **Add melodic decoration**

This is best done after checking that the inner parts are free of consecutives. The given passages indicate that this chorale, like most, has quaver movement on many beats, although not on all. It is never necessary to force decoration onto every beat – and the pause chord of the cadence should not normally be decorated at all.

It is best to keep to quavers for decoration. Bach *never* uses triplets – on the very few occasions when he needs a three-note pattern he uses the rhythm ♩♫ .

The simplest forms of melodic decoration are passing notes to link two pitches that are a 3rd apart and auxiliaries to link two notes of the same pitch. They should be chosen with a view to making the music flow better, and not just added for the sake of padding.

There is one final improvement to make. In Example 6.12.3 *above*, there is a perfect 5th between the two upper parts at the end of the first complete bar, followed by a diminished 5th (E and B♭) at the start of the next bar. Although this doesn't count as consecutive 5ths, we could disguise the parallelism by suspending the alto F so that it is delayed for a quaver, before resolving to E:

Ex: 6.12.4

7   Final check

Check that all of your chords are correct, any accidentals needed have been included (specially important in minor keys) and that there are no consecutives in any of the six pairs of parts (as listed at the top of page 53).

Make sure that your notation is clear. If you write 'blobby' notes like those shown *left* you cannot expect the examiner to give you the benefit of the doubt about which notes you mean – they will more likely be regarded as wrong notes.

Finally, erase or cross through any rough work that you do not want the examiner to mark.

Activity 6.12

Complete the alto and tenor parts at the cadences in the following chorale, so that there is four-part harmony throughout. (Adding inner parts in this way was a task that Bach used to set for his own students.) This is a relatively plain setting, so there will be little or no opportunity to add any further melodic decoration.

The third phrase is clearly in the dominant – you will find that the second phrase is much easier to harmonise if you treat it as also being in the dominant key.

Melody: Darmstadt, 1687

6.13 Spotting a modulation

In the previous activity, it was obvious that the third phrase modulated to E major because of the D♯–E in the given melody, supported by a V–I cadence pattern in E in the given bass part.

But it was not so clear that the second phrase modulated, and it would have been even less clear if the bass hadn't been given. This is because the tell-tale accidental (D♯) was not printed – it needs to occur in one or both of your added inner parts.

There is a clue, though. If the second phrase had stayed in A major, the G♯ in the melody would have been the leading-note and should therefore rise to the tonic, A. It doesn't – and that's a signal that the music may no longer be in A major.

You need to be alert for clues such as this, as most chorales are likely to include at least one phrase that modulates. In short chorales, such phrases usually end with a **perfect cadence in the new key**. The dominant or relative major are the most likely keys for a modulation, but any related key is possible. Look at the following short and simple chorale melody:

Ex: 6.13 Freylinghausen's *Gesangbuch*, 1704

At first sight this melody appears to be in D major throughout. But there are two clues as to why it should not be harmonised entirely in that key.

The first is again a leading-note in the melody (marked *) which fails to rise to the tonic. It is a sure sign of modulation and, since the phrase ends with 3–2–2–1 in the scale of A major, the dominant is the most likely key for the end of this second phrase.

The second clue is the melody at the third cadence. It consists of 3–4 in the scale of D major, and there is no cadence that would support that combination of pitches. We therefore need to think what else might be possible. V–I in G major (the subdominant key) would certainly work, but in fact it is actually harmonised by V–I in E minor, the relative minor of the subdominant.

There can often be a choice of keys for any given melody. For instance, the first phrase *above* could end with V–I in B minor. The choice depends on context. Here, the phrases are all short, and the very first cadence would really be too early for a modulation – so it is harmonised as a perfect cadence (actually *vii*b–I) in the tonic.

6.14 Practice tests in chorale cadences

We have provided four practice tasks in Activity **6.14**. To get you started, tasks (a) and (b) are rather simpler than those set in Edexcel AS Music exams, while (c) and (d) are similar in standard to those in the examination.

For additional practice you could add approach chords to the cadences you wrote for Activities **6.7** and **6.8**. You could also try completing four chords at each cadence in Exercise 6.13 *above*, noting the comments about modulations.

You may already know the melody of chorale (a) in the following activity as the hymn 'Now thank we all our God'. The two given cadences in this chorale are, unusually, both plagal. Think carefully about the key of the penultimate cadence. Would it sound better harmonised in C major or A minor?

In chorales (a), (c) and (d), watch out for places where the first chord of the cadence itself has a minim in the melody. These notes will needs enlivening with two different chords, or at least a suspension, to maintain interest.

Complete the cadences in each of the following four chorales.

(a)

Melody: Johann Crüger, 1647 (adapted)

(b)

Melody: Halle, 1704

This is an anticipation: do not harmonise it as a separate chord

(c)

Melody: HB

Note the double surprise in the second complete bar of chorale (d) – a very early shift to G minor and an interrupted cadence. The cadences you write should be perfect and imperfect. How will you treat the pair of quavers marked *? Is the E♭ a harmony note and the D a passing note, or is D the harmony note and E♭ therefore an *accented passing note*?

(d)

R101

6.15 Anacrusic openings and échappées

Before starting on complete chorales, there are a couple more techniques to learn about that are likely to be needed in more advanced work.

Anacrusic openings

Many chorale phrases begin with an **anacrusis** or up-beat. Sometimes an anacrusic start will suggest a progression such as V–I, shown at (i) in Example 6.15.1. However, in many cases Bach is perfectly happy to repeat an opening tonic chord on the first beat of the next bar, even when a V–I start would be possible, as shown in (ii).

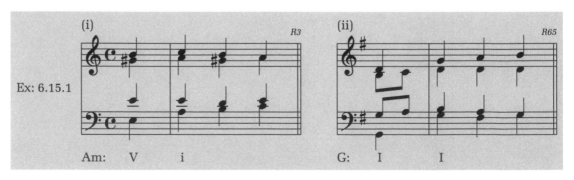

Ex: 6.15.1

This is an important exception to the rule that the same chord should not normally be repeated from a weak to a strong beat. However, note that Bach often includes an upward leap of an octave in the bass (as he does here) in order to give the down-beat chord greater rhythmic impetus.

Échappées

Although we have covered most kinds of melodic decoration, there is one further type that you may occasionally encounter. In the following example the note marked * is a dissonance known as an **échappée** or **escape note**. An échappée leaves a harmony note by step (usually upwards) before leaping in the opposite direction (usually by a 3rd) to a new harmony note:

Ex: 6.15.2

6.16 Harmonising a complete chorale melody

The chorales test for Edexcel A2 Music, and for some other exams, requires the completion of a complete chorale melody. While this involves more work than just adding a cadential progression, the basic method is the same. Indeed, it is often a good idea to start with the cadences first, and their approach chords, and then work back to the start of each phrase.

In this section we are going to work in order through the steps needed to harmonise the chorale melody in Example 6.16.1. As usual in harmonisation exercises, the first few beats have been completed for you – these are useful in indicating the style expected, particularly with regard to the amount of melodic decoration.

Ex: 6.16.1

1 Identify the keys throughout the exercise

In most cases you should expect the last phrase to be in the same key as the start of the chorale and for at least one of the phrases before the end to modulate and cadence in a related key.

In this chorale melody, there are no accidentals to suggest a specific modulation, but we should still expect to modulate in one of the phrases. Which one?

Three of the four phrases end with a fall of a 2nd. Those that finish G–F are clearly inviting perfect cadences in F major. But what about the phrase that ends D–C? Name a suitable related key that could support a perfect cadence on these two notes.

2   Identify each cadence, including approach chords, then write in the bass notes

This is similar to work we have done previously, so do this for yourself now, and then compare your answers to the suggestions below.

Phrase 1. The melody ends with 3–2–2–1 in F major, inviting a perfect cadence in the tonic. It is a good idea to harmonise the repeated Gs with two different chords and this could be done with the familiar pattern I–ii⁷b–V–I. The first chord I, with F in the bass, is virtually inevitable in view of the given leading-note (E) on the previous quaver, supporting chord V⁷b.

Phrase 2. The melody ends with 1–2, suggesting an imperfect cadence in the tonic, I–V. The two notes before the cadence, F and E, also suggest I–V, but I–V–I–V for the complete progression would be rather dull. One solution would be to include an inverted chord and to use *viib* instead of the first chord V. This gives Ib–*viib*–I–V, which works well and offers more interest.

Phrase 3. Hopefully you spotted that this phrase can modulate to the dominant – always the most likely choice for a modulation in major-key chorales. The cadence itself is therefore V–I in C major, and this could be approached by either IV or ii to harmonise the F in the melody. The E at the end of the previous bar could be supported by chord vi (A minor in this key), but a tonic chord of C major might be more helpful in defining the new key of C.

Phrase 4. This must end with a perfect cadence in F major. Notes 3–2–1 can be treated as Ic–V–I (although Ib–V–I would be just as good). To avoid using the tonic chord too many times, the F at the end of the previous bar can be harmonised with chord vi. This will still allow the alto to prepare the dissonant 4th (F) in chord Ic.

We now have the following skeleton harmonisation:

3   Choose chords for the first part of each phrase, and write in the bass notes

Work forwards from the beginning of a phrase until you reach the chords already chosen for the cadential progression. Be prepared to change one or more of the new chords in order to achieve a good join.

The first chord of a new phrase must lead on well from the preceding cadence. Where possible, repeat the pause chord, with an octave shift in the bass (see the change to bar 3 in the next example). It doesn't matter if this causes an overlap.

Here are reminders of several important points:

✦ I and V$^{(7)}$, and their inversions, are the most useful of all chords.

✦ Progressions in which the roots fall in 5ths (or rise in 4ths) are particularly strong. Chords with roots that fall in 3rds can also be very useful.

✦ Mix $\frac{5}{3}$ and $\frac{6}{3}$ chords rather than use many root-position chords in succession. The result is more varied, bass parts are usually less angular, and contrary motion between S and B is often easy to achieve.

✦ Modulations are usually best started early in the phrase, rather than left to the cadence itself. The cadence should merely confirm the new key.

With this advice in mind, try completing the remaining chords and bass notes. Compare your working with Example 6.16.3 *below* – but remember that there can be more than one right answer!

Notice that the bass minim on F in bar 3 has been moved down an octave. This is to allow the bass to rise to the upper F when the next phrase starts with the same chord. At the end of bar 5 we can't make a similar upward shift of an octave in the bass because this would take the bass part too high in the remainder of the phrase.

Ex: 6.16.3

4 Add inner parts and check everything

Here are a few pointers to adding the alto and tenor parts:

✦ In bar 2 the given G in the alto ends with a tie. This G must continue under the soprano A, producing a 9–8 suspension against the bass F. The tied G will then need to resolve to F on the second quaver of the second beat. This F can then form the preparation for the 7th (E) of chord ii^{7}b on the third beat.

✦ The first half of bar 4 is very much like the first half of bar 2 – it would be a good idea to make some difference between the two, perhaps by making one of the inner parts different.

✦ In the last bar, a 4–3 suspension in the alto (F–E) would fit well over chord V – the F can be prepared in the alto on the first beat of the bar. The resolution (E) is the leading note and this could then fall to C in the final chord, producing a very stylish perfect cadence.

After adding the inner parts, check all six combinations of parts for consecutives. Be specially careful at the start of the final phrase – two adjacent $\frac{5}{3}$ chords (I–ii), with outer parts in similar motion, are prone to consecutive 5ths, so try to ensure that the inner parts move in contrary motion to the bass at this point.

5   Add any further melodic decoration required

We can see from the given opening that this chorale, like many others, should contain quaver movement on most beats – although not all, and not during the pause chords.

In the final working below, the opportunity has been taken to add several passing notes, additional harmony notes (at the end of bar 4), a lower auxiliary (bass, in the last bar) and some additional suspensions.

After adding notes of melodic decoration, always check that they have not introduced consecutives where there were none before.

Ex: 6.16.4

Example 6.16.4 is a completed harmonisation of the melody shown in Example 6.16.1 – it is not exactly what Bach wrote, which is more elaborate, but it shows a clear understanding of Bach's musical 'grammar' and style, and would therefore achieve a good mark in an exam.

There are two final points to note.

✦ In the second half of bar 6, the dotted note in the alto means that D continues to sound against the chord of C on the last beat, creating a 9–8 suspension. The preparation, suspension and resolution (all in the alto) are marked P, S and R.

✦ We decided that the last cadence should be Ic–V–I. When using Ic the 5th should be doubled, so C appears in both T and B at the start of the final bar. Also, the 4th above the bass in Ic needs to be resolved (and, whenever possible, prepared) in the same part.

Here the 4th above the bass is the note F in the alto at the start of the last bar. It is prepared by the alto F at the end of the previous bar and is resolved by the alto E on the second beat of the last bar. E is the leading note and, at a cadence, should generally fall directly to the dominant in the tonic chord to sound really stylish. This characteristic pattern of preparation, 4th, resolution and fall is marked P, 4, R and F in Example 6.16.4.

Activity 6.16

(a) Play and study Example 6.16.4 *opposite*.

(b) If you have access to a copy of *Riemenschneider*, compare Example 6.16.4 with Bach's own settings of this chorale – *R68* in F major and *R247* in G major.

You can learn a lot from comparing Bach's two settings with each other and with our own harmonisation here. *R68* and *R247* are both a bit more elaborate than would reasonably be expected in a chorale test – but remember that Bach is often more ambitious and/or imaginative than we can normally hope to be.

Why do you think that Bach found it necessary to cross the alto and tenor parts at the start of bar 5 in *R68*?

6.17 Practice tests in harmonising complete chorale melodies

The first two practice tasks are a little simpler than the exercises normally set in exams. The melody of the chorale in (a) is quite widely sung as a hymn in Britain.

Activity 6.17.1

(a) Complete the harmonisation of the following chorale melody. Remember to include some passing notes and possibly other types of melodic decoration.

Tip 1 The melody in bar 5 starts with the ascending scale pattern, 1–2–3. This is very common in chorales, and can be effectively harmonised with the progression Ib–*viib*–I. If the reverse of this pattern (notes 3–2–1) occurs *early in the phrase*, it can be harmonised with the same three chords in reverse order: I–*viib*–Ib. The contrary motion between S and B is excellent in both cases. This harmonisation is well worth remembering since it can be used in many chorales.

Musikalisches Handbuch, Hamburg, 1690 (adapted)

Tip 2 The melody of the final cadence in this chorale consists of another common pattern, the pitches 8–8–7–8. This is often harmonised with vi–ii^{7}b–V–I, since the 7th of ii^{7}b appears in the soprano, and can be prepared in chord vi and resolved in chord V. But vi–Ic–V–I works equally well. In this case it is the 4th of chord Ic that is prepared and resolved in the soprano. Try out both progressions.

(b) Complete the harmonisation of the following chorale melody, adding passing notes where appropriate.

The second phrase ends with 8–8–7–8 (notice the change of key) – re-read the last paragraph on the previous page for ways in which to harmonise this pattern.

The ending of the third phrase could be treated as notes 3–2 in F major or notes 2–1 in G minor. Which do you think works better in this chorale, bearing in mind what follows in the final phrase?

Melody from Koch's *Choralbuch*, 1816

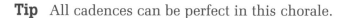

The tasks in Activity 6.17.2 *below* don't need to be tackled in a single sitting. They will test your knowledge of Bach's style of chorale harmonisation rather more fully. The final one is a little longer than most exam exercises.

Activity 6.17.2

(a) Complete the harmonisation of the following chorale melody.

Tip All cadences can be perfect in this chorale.

R6 (adapted)

(b) This chorale is quite short, but each phrase is unusually long. It passes through C major in bar 2, but is otherwise entirely in A minor.

(c) In a chorale melody the second of each pair of quavers is usually a passing note. However, the note marked * *below* should be treated as a lower auxiliary, and it is best to harmonise the two quavers at the end of this bar with separate chords.

Note the harmonisation of the soprano's minim D in bar 2. The chord on the first beat of the bar is ii^7 (whose 7th, A, is prepared in the tenor at the end of bar 1). As the soprano sustains the D, the chord changes on the second beat of the bar to V^7. Will this cadence, transposed to E major, work in bar 4?

There is a large-scale melodic repeat in this exercise. Aim for some harmonic variety in the repeated phrases (but avoid anything out of style).

(d) Complete the three lower parts in the following chorale. It is longer than you would normally expect in an exam question, so don't worry if you don't complete it all. There are also several tricky moments – here are some tips:

✦ If you are unsure how to tackle the ends of phrases 4 and 8, consider the possibility of imperfect cadences in C minor.

✦ Bach unusually uses a minim in all parts on the first note (E♭) of phrase 6, probably because the word in the chorale text at this point is 'peace'.

✦ There is an anticipation before the final note of the cadence at the end of phrase 6. This should not be harmonised separately.

R215 (omitting last two phrases)

6.18 Tricky phrase endings

Many of the phrases endings in chorales fall into one of the common patterns we have encountered in this chapter. Occasionally you may encounter other patterns, although exam questions don't usually include anything really non-standard.

To see how Bach treats less common melodic patterns, play and analyse the cadences at the end of the following phrases:

✦ *R65*, phrases 3 and 4 – harmonising falling 5ths in the melody. Compare the same phrases in his other setting of the same chorale in *R293* and also look at *R332*, phrase 2, which similarly ends with a falling 5th,

✦ *R95*, phrases 1, 5 and 6 – harmonising a repeated note at the end of the cadence. Compare these with *R128*, phrases 1, 2, 4 and 5, in which Bach uses repeated chords to harmonise falling melodic 3rds at the end of the cadence.

6.19 Chorale harmonisation in triple time

If you should have to work a chorale in $\frac{3}{4}$ time, don't panic! The progressions and style of part-writing are the same as in common time. There are just three points to bear in mind:

✦ Sometimes the melody moves in a succession of minims and crotchets, with many of the minims taking a single chord.

✦ Passing notes below the minims are therefore crotchets rather than quavers.

✦ Some phrases may end with a **hemiola** immediately before the last chord of the cadence. This gives the effect of three minim beats in the space of two bars of $\frac{3}{4}$ time, and is most commonly seen when the prevailing pattern of | ♩ ♩ | ♩ ♩ | is replaced by a pattern such as | ♩ ♩ | ♩♩ | before the last chord of the phrase as shown *below*.

Example 6.19 (i) illustrates all three of these points. If you compare it with (ii), you can see that working in $\frac{3}{4}$ time is otherwise no different to working in common time.

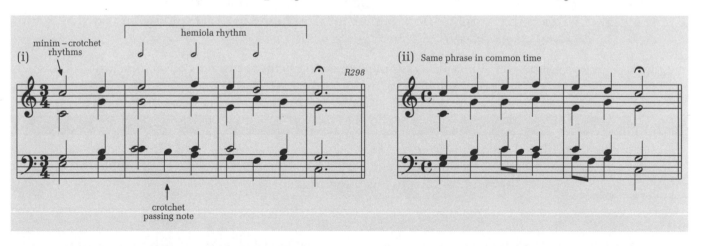

Activity 6.19

Complete the lower parts of the chorale at the top of the next page. While it would be possible to harmonise it all in the tonic key, see if you can introduce some variety by modulating to the relative minor at the end of the third phrase.

If you are feeling confident, you could consider using secondary dominant chords in the second phrase. Bach used V of vi and V^7 of V in this phrase, again with the aim of providing some harmonic variety for a melody which employs the same rhythm in every phrase.

R334 (transposed)

6.20 Addition of three upper parts to a bass

Some types of chorale tests, such as those in WJEC A2 Music, include some phrases in which a bass part is given, often with figures, rather than the chorale melody. The figuring identifies the chords to be used. For more on figured bass, see Sections **7.1 – 7.3** and **7.13** in the next chapter.

Begin by adding the soprano, in agreement with the figuring if any is given. Chorale melodies can go as high as G at the top of the treble stave, or as low as B below the stave, but they often lie between D above middle C and E an octave above, and any one melody seldom exceeds a range of a 9th.

Most movement in chorale melodies tends to be stepwise and the largest leaps (which are rarely greater than a perfect 5th) are found between phrases rather than within any single phrase.

When the soprano is complete check that there are no consecutives with the given bass. Then add the alto and tenor parts, again being careful to observe any figuring.

Activity 6.20

Add soprano, alto and tenor parts above the bass in each of the following phrases. Make sure you follow the given figuring in (i).

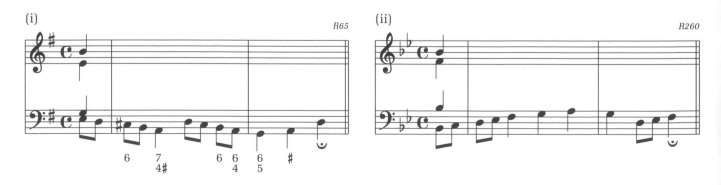

(i)   R65   (ii)   R260

7 Baroque counterpoint

Baroque counterpoint exercises are normally based on music written between about 1680 and 1750. We covered the basics of counterpoint in Chapter 5, which you must work through before starting this chapter. Here we will learn about

✦ Figured bass – the system of symbols used by composers of this period to indicate chords

✦ Adding a single melody part above a given figured bass – an option in Edexcel AS and A2 Music exams

✦ Completing three-part (trio-sonata) textures with figured bass – an option for the WJEC A2 Music exam

✦ Completing two-part keyboard exercises (not involving figured bass) by adding a part to a given part – an option for the OCR A2 Music exam.

If you are studying for the OCR option, you do not need to know about figured bass, but you should work through Sections **7.5** to **7.8** before turning to Section **7.12**, which deals more specifically with the OCR style of test.

7.1 Figured bass

A **figured bass** is a bass part in baroque music which includes numbers and other symbols (such as sharp and flat signs) below the notes. These show the types of chords required, enabling a keyboard (or lute) player to improvise an accompaniment for other fully-notated parts. This process is known as **realising** a figured bass.

In practice, baroque composers tended to rely on the players' experience to know what chords were needed from the context of the bass part alone, and so often used figures only where there might be any uncertainty. But in exams the bass part is normally figured sufficiently fully to avoid any doubt about the chords required.

Ex. 7.1

Figured bass works purely in terms of **intervals above the bass**, using the scale of the current key. So, in Example 7.1 the figures $^6_4$ indicate that a 4th and a 6th above G are required to complete the chord, thus making a $^6_4$ chord of C major. The player has considerable freedom to adapt the realisation to the context, providing that the basic chord is correct. The notes may be put in different octaves, some may be doubled, the chord might be arpeggiated, and passing notes and other types of melodic decoration might be improvised to link a progression of chords.

7.2 Figured bass: using numbers

Baroque composers and players were so familiar with the figured bass system that abbreviated figuring was used whenever possible. In particular, the figures 5 and 3 were not used unless needed for clarification. So, where a $^5_3$ (the most common type of chord) was required, no figures at all were used.

Widely-used figurings are listed in the following table. The first column shows the abbreviated figuring, which is what you should normally expect to see. The second column shows the full figuring, and the third column gives descriptions and examples (all in close position). You don't need to learn this table by heart. Providing you know your intervals and keys, and understand how figuring is abbreviated, you can always work out the required notes directly from the figured bass part.

Any of the figurings in the following table may appear in Edexcel tests at A2 level, but you will not be required to used those marked * in Edexcel AS tests.

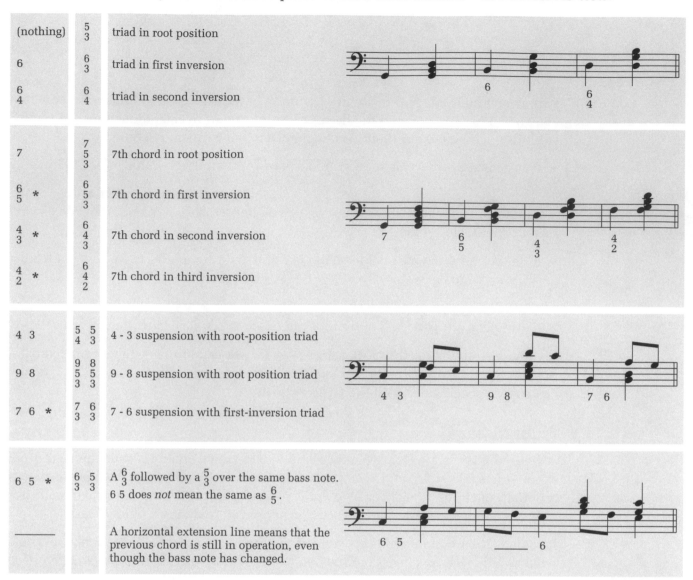

(nothing)	$\begin{smallmatrix}5\\3\end{smallmatrix}$	triad in root position
6	$\begin{smallmatrix}6\\3\end{smallmatrix}$	triad in first inversion
$\begin{smallmatrix}6\\4\end{smallmatrix}$	$\begin{smallmatrix}6\\4\end{smallmatrix}$	triad in second inversion
7	$\begin{smallmatrix}7\\5\\3\end{smallmatrix}$	7th chord in root position
$\begin{smallmatrix}6\\5\end{smallmatrix}$ *	$\begin{smallmatrix}6\\5\\3\end{smallmatrix}$	7th chord in first inversion
$\begin{smallmatrix}4\\3\end{smallmatrix}$ *	$\begin{smallmatrix}6\\4\\3\end{smallmatrix}$	7th chord in second inversion
$\begin{smallmatrix}4\\2\end{smallmatrix}$ *	$\begin{smallmatrix}6\\4\\2\end{smallmatrix}$	7th chord in third inversion
4 3	$\begin{smallmatrix}5\\4\end{smallmatrix}$ $\begin{smallmatrix}5\\3\end{smallmatrix}$	4 - 3 suspension with root-position triad
9 8	$\begin{smallmatrix}9\\5\\3\end{smallmatrix}$ $\begin{smallmatrix}8\\5\\3\end{smallmatrix}$	9 - 8 suspension with root position triad
7 6 *	$\begin{smallmatrix}7\\3\end{smallmatrix}$ $\begin{smallmatrix}6\\3\end{smallmatrix}$	7 - 6 suspension with first-inversion triad
6 5 *	$\begin{smallmatrix}6\\3\end{smallmatrix}$ $\begin{smallmatrix}5\\3\end{smallmatrix}$	A $\begin{smallmatrix}6\\3\end{smallmatrix}$ followed by a $\begin{smallmatrix}5\\3\end{smallmatrix}$ over the same bass note. 6 5 does *not* mean the same as $\begin{smallmatrix}6\\5\end{smallmatrix}$.
_____		A horizontal extension line means that the previous chord is still in operation, even though the bass note has changed.

Activity 7.2

(a) Add figuring where needed under each of the following chords.

(b) Add notes above the following bass part to make the chords indicated by the figuring. The first three chords have been completed for you.

7.3 Figured bass: using accidentals

Figuring works in connection with the key signature. The first example *below* has no figuring, so it must be a $\frac{5}{3}$ chord on E. Since the key signature contains a G♯, the notes of this $\frac{5}{3}$ are E–G♯–B, a triad of E major. The second example does not have a G♯ in the key signature, so this $\frac{5}{3}$ must be E–G–B, a triad of E minor.

In order to change any pitches dictated by the key signature, accidentals are needed in the figuring. **An accidental by itself alters the 3rd of the chord.** So in the next two examples, the first chord is E minor and the second is E major.

The most common use of an accidental is to accommodate the raised leading note in a minor key, as in Example 7.3.2 (ii), where G♯ is the leading note of A minor.

Many Edexcel exam questions have used ♯3, ♮3 and ♭3 instead of just ♯, ♮ or ♭, but the meaning is exactly the same, since an accidental *with* a number changes the pitch of that particular note number. For instance, in Example 7.3.3:

✦ ♭5 means that the 5th above the bass must be flattened, and
✦ ♯6 means that the 6th above the bass must be sharpened – and so on.

Finally, note that in some printed music the accidental is written *after* the numeral (for instance, 6♭ instead of ♭6) and that sharpening is indicated by a slash through a number instead of by an accidental – for example, 6̸ means the same as ♯6.

Activity 7.3

(a) Write the correct figuring below the stave for each of the following chords.

(b) Write a chord in close position over each of the following bass notes to match the following figurings. The first chord is given.

7.4 Two-part texture

A figured bass tells you which chords are required, but when you add a melody to a given bass, only one note at a time can sound above the bass part. Therefore you will have to choose suitable notes from the chords in order to create your melody:

✦ Where there is no figuring the chord is a $\frac{5}{3}$ and so you can choose a 5th above the bass, or a 3rd, or even an octave – but **a 3rd is usually preferred**

✦ Where the only figuring is a 6, the chord is a $\frac{6}{3}$ and so you can choose a 6th above the bass, or a 3rd, or even an octave – **6ths and 3rds are both widely used**

✦ Within these constraints, pitches should be selected to give a good melodic shape and to develop the style of the given material.

In the following figured bass a start has been made by writing down the available notes for each new chord the first time it appears:

Next, notes are selected from these chords with a view to creating pleasing melodic shapes – falling towards the end of the first phrase, and rising in the second. A rest has been used to separate the phrases, its position determined by the V–I bass (D–G) in bar 2^{2-3}, which can serve as a perfect cadence at the end of the first phrase:

Finally, this skeleton melody is clothed with some distinctive rhythms, taking us to what the composer actually wrote. Further notes (additional harmony notes) have been added from the original chords, plus a passing note on A in bar 2:

As in most baroque two-part writing, the majority of intervals here are 3rds. There are a few 6ths (on some of the chords that are figured 6). There are several octaves, but most are tucked away on weak semiquavers. An octave can sound too bare on the beat, although there is nothing better at the end of a strong perfect cadence to reinforce note 1. Toom nay 5ths on strong beats can seem bare and ambiguous (neither major or minor). In Example 7.4.3 Telemann is happy to start with a 5th, but he wouldn't end on one. As Baroque composers often do, he uses a prominent 5th on chord V of the perfect cadence in bar 2^2, leading to an octave on G at the end of the phrase.

(a) Work out the notes needed for the chords in the following figured bass. Then add a melody in the same rhythm, choosing one note from each chord.

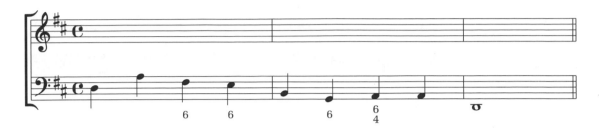

(b) Copy out this figured bass on a sheet of manuscript paper, and then add *two* different notes in succession above most of the given notes. For instance, you might start with F♯–A quavers above the first note. Keep mainly to the notes of the chords, but add a passing note or two if you wish.

7.5 Melodic decoration

On the opposite page we saw how additional harmony notes and a passing note were used to give musical interest to the basic structure of a melody. Melodic decoration is an important feature of baroque music. Patterns are formed from notes of the current chord (harmony notes) along with the following types of decoration:

◆ Passing notes (P)
◆ Accented passing notes (APN)
◆ Auxiliary notes (AUX).

In the following examples, non-harmony notes are printed in lighter type:

You are also likely to encounter:

◆ Anticipations (ANT)
◆ Échappées (É) – see page 91 for an explanation of this decoration.

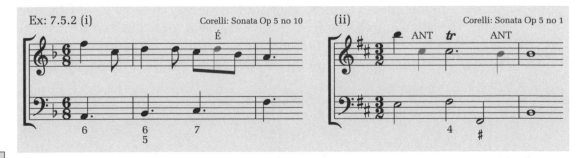

Non-harmony notes should always be approached by step from the previous note and (apart from the leap after an échappée) should move by step to the next note.

You shouldn't expect to add any slurs, dynamics or marks of articulation (such as staccato dots) unless such things are printed in the given material – in which case, use that as a model. However, there is one symbol that is often worth including. When the melody at a cadence falls from 2 to 1, or rises from 7 to 8, it is very common in baroque music for note 2 or note 7 to be decorated with a trill. A trill is just another type of melodic decoration, but instead of writing out the notes required you just need to add the symbol *tr* above the note concerned, as in Example 7.5.2 (ii).

Using the abbreviations on the previous page, label each decoration marked *.

Corelli: Sonata Op 5 no 8

7.6 Using dissonant harmonic intervals

The types of melodic decoration outlined in the previous section are *not* shown in the figuring – they are for you to add. However, if your melody includes suspensions or 7ths indicated by the figuring, **such dissonances must be prepared and resolved**.

Example 7.6.1 (i) *below* shows the correct preparation and resolution of a 7th chord (ii^7 in B♭ major). In (ii) the 7th over the C has been neither prepared nor resolved and is therefore wrong. Part (iii) of the example shows the correct preparation and suspension of a 4–3 suspension, while (iv) shows the same suspension treated incorrectly, since it has neither preparation nor resolution.

Ex: 7.6.1

Including figured dissonances in your added part can be quite a time-saver. In (i) *above*, can you see how writing a 7th above the bass note figured 7 gives three notes for the price of one? This is because a B♭ must precede the dissonant B♭ (to prepare it) and an A must follow the dissonant B♭ (to resolve it).

Sometimes it is impossible for the melody to reflect *every* figured dissonance. In the next example, the first 7th (G) has been included, but its resolution to F♯ gets in the way of including the second 7th – it must be assumed that the harpsichord player will incorporate it in the realisation, perhaps as shown by the small notes:

Ex. 7.6.2

This activity is about the preparation and resolution of dissonances. Add the notes missing from the following passages. In (iii) remember that it may not be possible to reflect every dissonance in the added part.

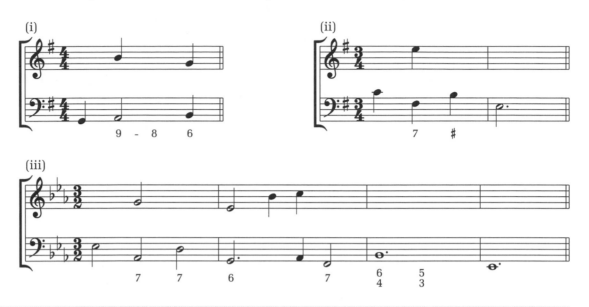

7.7 Cadences and modulation in figured basses

You might be tempted to think that figured bass is mostly about playing with numbers. True, you don't have to choose chords as in chorale harmonisation, but if you're to build a coherent melodic line you must know where cadences are implied. You must also be able to identify modulations, if only to know what accidentals are necessary.

The progression ivb–V in a minor key is known as a phrygian cadence – see page 77.

In early 18th-century baroque counterpoint **the majority of cadences are perfect**. Many involve a drop of an octave in the bass from upper dominant to lower dominant, followed by the rise of a 4th to the tonic. If the bass of a minor-key phrase, or even a whole exercise, ends with a falling minor 2nd, the cadence is imperfect (ivb–V).

Modulations are sometimes clear from accidentals in the bass part, but also look for accidentals in the figuring. The first sign of D major in Example 7.4.1 on page 104 is the ♯ before the figure 6 in the third bar.

Play the following bass. Name the modulation(s) indicated by accidentals on the stave and/or in the figuring. Locate and name the three cadences.

Handel: Sonata No 4 in D minor

7.8 Imitation and the use of rests

See Section **5.4** on pages 66–67 for more on imitation.

Some baroque two-part writing features imitation, although often not exact and rarely for longer than a few notes at a time. If you use imitation, remember that it must make good harmonic sense with the given part and must not contradict the figuring.

Finding where imitation will fit is a matter of trial and error. It should sit easily with the metre of the music – for example, in $\frac{4}{4}$ time the imitation is much more likely to enter two or four beats behind or ahead of the given part than at three beats' distance. An imitating part is frequently an octave, 4th or 5th above or below the other part, which often helps to emphasise notes 1 and 5. Both of these points are illustrated in Example 7.8.1 (i) *below*.

There may be rests in the bass when imitation is expected to occur in the added part, as in Example 7.8.1 (i). These help to highlight the imitation. Here are a few more tips on the use of rests:

✦ Never write a rest simply because you can't think of a note to write!

✦ Short rests (up to one beat) can occur at the same time in both parts, to help articulate the music (as in bar 2 of Example 7.9.1 on page 110)

✦ Rests longer than one beat are best avoided in an added top part, except perhaps before an imitative entry

✦ When there is a rest in the bass between identical chords, the added part above the rest should fit with that chord, as in (i) *below*. If the harmony changes after the rest, the added part may instead fit with the new chord, as in (ii):

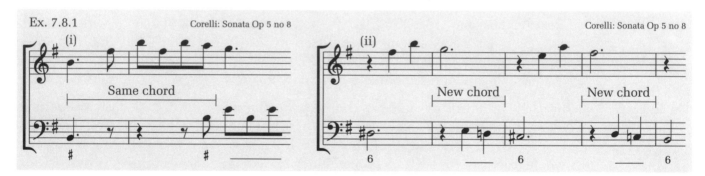

Ex. 7.8.1   Corelli: Sonata Op 5 no 8   Corelli: Sonata Op 5 no 8

Let's see how a violin part can be added to the following figured bass. The violin should enter at the start, since there's no point in beginning with rests in both parts.

Ex. 7.8.2

The rests are a strong clue that when the bass enters it imitates the violin. If the violin starts with the bass melody an octave higher the notes A–D will establish D minor from the outset by implying V–I. Imitation works up to the first note of bar 2, after which Corelli cunningly continues with the opening of bar 1, an octave higher:

Ex. 7.8.3   Corelli: Sonata Op 5 no 8

(a) Complete the top part in the following, using imitation. Remember that the rests in the bass part (and the given rest on the top stave) provide clues as to where imitative entries may occur.

Thorley: *Flute piece*

(b) This task is designed for OCR candidates. If you are taking the Edexcel exam you will not be required to add a bass part to a melody.

Complete the bass in the following, starting with an imitative entry. Begin by working out where the bass should enter and on what note. If you get this right, you should be able to keep the imitation going for several bars.

Corelli: Sonata Op 5, no 7

If you are taking the OCR exam you should now turn to Section **7.12**.

7.9 Working an Edexcel AS exercise

Introduction

The given material always includes a complete bass part with figuring. The opening of the top part is provided to show the style and act as a model, and sometimes other passages in the melody may be given. You have to complete the top part according to the figuring and in an appropriate style.

You are not expected to know the tiny differences of style between different baroque composers. But do build up a broad knowledge of late-baroque style by playing and listening to plenty of sonatas by such composers as Corelli, Handel, Telemann and Vivaldi. (Bach's music has not been set by Edexcel for this question.)

Here is a method for working an AS exercise:

1 **Choose an instrument** (from a given list) to play the top part – there is advice about the range and characterstics of various instruments on page 176

2 **Identify key(s) and cadence points**

3 **Make an outline for the top part** by writing in pitches and/or rhythms where they seem obvious

4 **Complete your top part**, by adding to and elaborating your outline

5 **Check your work** for consecutives and correct treatment of dissonances, and to ensure that you have observed (and not contradicted) the given figuring.

Play and study the following music:

Ex. 7.9.1

Telemann: Sonatina II

Step 1 Possible instruments for the top part are violin, flute or oboe. We will choose violin.

Step 2 The music begins and ends in B♭ major. It visits F major at the end of the first half and later passes through G minor (shown by the F♯–D–G pattern in bars 11–12).

We hear decisive perfect cadences in bars 7–8 (F major) and 15–16 (B♭ major). In addition, the bass outlines an inverted perfect cadence in bars 3–4 (Vb–I in B♭ major) and a perfect cadence in G minor (the pattern in bars 11–12 mentioned *above*).

Early 18th-century composers generally preferred not to over-emphasise a cadence in the middle of a section. So, although the 16 bars form a regular structure of four four-bar phrases, we'll try to keep the added part moving at bars 3–4 and 10–11 rather than let it come to a halt on a long note.

Step 3 The figuring gives much guidance for building a melodic outline, but also look for:

✦ Sequence or straight repetition in the given material

✦ Clues at points where the given sections of the melody end

✦ Obvious notes at cadence points.

Notice first that the bass part of bars 1–2 is repeated a 5th higher in bars 9–10. The top part should be transposed similarly – although it will match up with bar 11 better if it is transposed down a 4th than up a 5th.

Now look for clues at points where the given material ends, and at cadences. We can:

✦ Add D in bar 4 since the E♭ at the end of the previous bar is clearly a passing note – write it as just a note head since we don't yet know how long it should be

✦ Add B♭ to fill bar 16 – since it's always good to end a piece on note 1 when there is a clear perfect cadence

✦ Add quaver rests at the ends of bars 6 and 10 to match those in bars 2 and 14

✦ In bar 15 the figuring suggests either D falling to C, or B♭ falling to A, on the last two quavers of the bar – both work well so we will choose the first solution.

Now see if there's anything in the given material that could be recycled to help create a stylistically unified working:

◆ Bars 13–14 could be adapted to fit the chords of bars 5–6. This has the advantage that each of the four phrases then begins with the same rhythm set to different rising triadic figures. Starting on A in bar 5 would work well, since it harmonises nicely with the bass, but starting the figure on F might also be a possibility.

Here is the stage we have now reached, with the notes and rests added in Step 3 printed in lighter type:

Ex. 7.9.2

Telemann: Sonatina II

Step 4   What we've added so far is very similar in style to the given material. We must keep this in mind as we work Step 4. We want the finished exercise to sound like one piece – not as if only parts of it are by an 18th-century composer!

Often the best way to fill a gap is by stepwise movement. An obvious example is the first note of bar 15, where E♭ can bridge the gap between F and D, and will harmonise with the E♭ in the bass. Don't worry that this leaves a bare octave on the first beat of bar 15 – this is not really a strong beat because bars 14–15 make up a hemiola (see Section **6.19** on page 99).

This leaves only bars 4 and 11–12 to complete. In both cases Telemann employed similar scalic figures, using melodic decoration to create stepwise movement. Look at bars 4 and 12 in the finished version *below* and note the use of upper auxiliaries (E♭ in bar 4 and C in bar 12) and passing notes.

Ex. 7.9.3

Telemann: Sonatina II

There are three final points to notice in Example 7.9.3:

✦ The fourth note in bar 11 (B♭) is an accented passing note which briefly contradicts the figuring, but immediately resolves to A. Although such very brief on-the-beat contradictions can be effective, avoid them if in doubt.

✦ The unprepared 7th at the start of bar 11 is a rare exception to the rule about preparing dissonances and is best avoided in your own work.

✦ At the end of bar 15 there is a semiquaver anticipation of the final B♭. The anticipation of the tonic at a cadence after notes 2 or 7 is a feature of baroque style.

Step 5   After working an exercise, make a thorough check. Don't feel demoralised if, as a result, you have to revise parts that you thought were complete. It's all part of the learning process. Here are the main things to check for:

✦ Has the figuring been followed correctly, including the correct preparation and resolution of any dissonances?

✦ Does each note 7 rise to 8 (unless in a falling scale passage)? But remember:

   ✦ Note 7 can fall if it is part of a descending scale, as in bar 3 of Example 7.9.3, where A is note 7 in the key of B♭ major.

   ✦ The rise to note 8 may be delayed, as in bar 5 of Example 7.9.3, where the A doesn't reach B♭ until the first beat of bar 6.

   ✦ If you have also been studying chorales, be aware that Bach's preference for a direct fall from 7 to 5 at chorale cadences does *not* extend to baroque two-part counterpoint.

✦ Are there any consecutive 5ths and octaves? Blatant on-the-beat consecutives are easy to spot in two-part writing! Some good news – octaves or 5ths between weak parts of neighbouring beats do *not* count as consecutives. Telemann was happy with the octaves shown in the following example because what we really hear is a sequence with parallel 3rds at the start of each bar.

Ex. 7.9.4

Telemann: Sonatina II

✦ Is the added part similar in style to the given material, perhaps even reusing some of its melodic and rhythmic patterns, as we did on the previous page? Be suspicious if your melody has a very different rhythmic character from the given opening. For instance, strings of quavers wouldn't work well in Example 7.9.3.

✦ Does each phrase of the completed melody have a pleasing overall shape? Many baroque phrases are basically arch-shaped, with the highest note somewhere in the middle.

✦ Have you used a reasonably large part of the instrument's available range? The melody in Example 7.9.3 has a range of one and half octaves – it doesn't use the violin's low or high registers, but the range is enough to give the melody variety and interest. Melodies that mainly hang around the same few pitches are unlikely to sound convincing.

Here is a set of practice exercises in the style of AS tests. In each one complete the top part in accordance with the given figuring, and in an appropriate style.

(a) Write for violin, flute, recorder or oboe – indicate your choice.

J C Fischer, Menuett No 15

(b) This is more of the sonatina by Telemann shown on page 104. Write for violin and try to continue in the same melodic and rhythmic style as Example 7.4.3.

Telemann: Sonatina in G

(c) Write for violin, flute, recorder or oboe – indicate your choice.

This is a sarabande, with a characteristic emphasis on the second beat in many bars. If you include the 9ths in bars 10 and 18, or the 4th in bar 19, be sure to prepare and resolve them in your added part.

J-C Naudot

(d) Write for violin in this extract.

Telemann: Sonatina VI

The figuring ♭6 in the first bar of the last stave above produces a first inversion of the triad on the flat supertonic, a chord known as a **Neapolitan 6th** – in the key of D minor that is a chord of E♭ major in first inversion (G–B♭–E♭). Put the distinctive E♭ in the melody, not the more ordinary B♭.

(e) Write for flute, oboe or violin and indicate your choice.

Handel: Sonata in D minor

7.10 Working an Edexcel A2 exercise

Exercises for A2 are longer than for AS, include a wider range of figurings, tend to be more elaborate in style and are more likely to involve imitation. However, the method for tackling these exercises follows the same five steps we followed in the previous section. Play and study the following music:

Ex. 7.10.1

Step 1   The list of possible instruments for the top part is violin, flute or oboe. The given passages could be played by any of them. Let's choose flute this time.

Step 2   Remember to take account of accidentals both in the bass and in the figuring when identifying keys. For example, a glance at C major in bar 3 is signalled both by the figuring on the first beat of the bar and the F♮ in the bass during the second beat.

In bars 4–5 the presence of both F♮ and B♭ signifies a brief modulation to F major – can you see where the figuring indicates V–Ib in this key in bar 4? This is unusual – F major is the subdominant of the subdominant – not one of the usual related keys. However, the key at the end of the first section (bar 7) is entirely standard.

The accidentals in bars 8–9, 12 and 16 signify secondary dominant chords rather than real modulations. Bar 8 contains V^7 of C followed by a chord of C itself, and bar 9 follows it in sequence – V^7 of D followed by a chord of D. There is a surprising chromatic twist in bar 17 – make sure you work out the chords carefully here.

There are also several clear perfect cadences, each with an octave drop in the bass. Mark all the points covered in Step 2 into the score.

Step 3   Next we need to create a melodic outline. The exercise contains several sequences and these are a real gift where a given phrase can be recycled at a different pitch. This is the case in bars 7^4–8^3 – just transpose it up a step and write it into bars 8^4–9^3, adjusting accidentals to match the new context.

With some sequences you will need to be more inventive. For instance, you must devise your own violin part in bar 3 before you repeat it in sequence in bar 4. You may well spot other places that could be treated sequentially, although the figuring may dictate that they won't work without some variation in the melody.

Always look for clues in the figuring. In bar 15 a 7th is needed above E, so sketch a D into the melody and resolve it to C on beat 2. This then provides the preparation for the 7th above D on beat 3 – sketch it in and resolve it to B on the last beat. Each of these two-beat pairs could take the same decorative treatment as the second half of bar 14 – and so another sequence has been created!

Look for other such opportunities – you could sketch in the 4–3 progression at the start of bar 13 (G–F♯). Remember that 4ths above the bass need preparation, so the G should also appear at the end of bar 12. The perfect cadences in bars 7 and 18 will probably end with the scale degree patterns 7–8 or 2–1.

Next, draft a few notes to fit bar 3 and their sequential repetition in bar 4, and experiment with ideas to fit the tricky harmony in bar 17. Remember that the 7th at the end of bar 16 (C) will need to resolve down a step, and the figuring therefore dictates that B♭ will be the first note of bar 17.

Before continuing, make sure you have sketched in all of the melodic ideas suggested in the course of Step 3.

Step 4   Now fill out your skeleton melody to produce a complete version. Your melody should reflect the style of the given material, so there should be plenty of quaver and semi-quaver movement, produced with the aid of melodic decoration. Notice that the notes in the given opening are entirely conjunct, apart from the leap after the rest in bar 1. This suggests that you, too, should aim for plenty of stepwise movement – but not entirely so, since there are leaps in the given melody in bars 11 and 14.

Step 5   Finally, check your work for consecutives, correct treatment of dissonances and consistency with the figuring, and the various other points listed on page 112.

Here is one possible working of Example 7.10.1. It is not as elaborate as Vivaldi's original (which is for violin), but it is a correct and reasonably stylish answer of the kind you should be aiming for. Notice the **octave displacement** on the first beats of bars 3 and 4, where a note is shifted an octave from its expected pitch to prevent the melody from getting too high – it is hardly ever necessary for the added part to extend more than about two octaves above middle C. Also note the imitation in bars 5–6.

Ex. 7.10.2

Complete the top part in each of the following passages, in accordance with the given figuring, and in an appropriate style.

(a) Write for violin, flute, recorder or oboe – indicate your choice. The time signature $\frac{3}{2}$ indicates a minim beat. Your added part should contain some crotchets but there is no need for quavers or semiquavers.

Notice that the music ends with a phrygian cadence and that there is a prominent hemiola in the two bars before the final chord.

(b) Write for violin. There is imitation between the parts in several places and notice that this excerpt ends in the dominant key.

Vivaldi: Sonata FXIII, no 31 (adapted)

(c) Write for violin, flute or oboe – indicate your choice. The music is a sarabande, with the expected emphasis on the second beat in some bars. Most phrases are four bars in length, but cadences are not always obvious as the bass (and the melody in the original) continues through most cadences, as in bars 3–4.

Jones: Suite No 1

7.11 Baroque trio sonatas (WJEC)

This section is for those studying for exams, such as WJEC A2 Music, in which the baroque counterpoint option requires the completion of *two* upper parts above a given figured bass. This three-part texture is most commonly found in trio sonatas – a type of chamber music much favoured in the baroque period, especially by Corelli (1653–1713), whose trio sonatas are for two violins with a figured bass part.

Extracts from Corelli's violin sonatas have already featured in this chapter, and the style of his trio sonatas is similar, although the use of a second violin part often provides more opportunities to use imitation. Example 7.11 *opposite* illustrates several other important features of Corelli's trio-sonata style:

✦ **The violin parts are close together and far above the bass** – the large gap between is filled by the realisation of the figured bass on a chordal instrument

✦ **The two violin parts often cross** (as in bars 9–12)

✦ The music is enlivened by **frequent clashes of a 2nd between the violins**, resolving to a 3rd (often with an ornamental resolution). Clashing 2nds may result from

   ✦ **4–3 suspensions** above the bass, as in bar 4

   ✦ **9–8 suspensions** above the bass, as in bar 3 (note how the first violin jumps to the harmony note F before resolving the suspended C to B♭)

   ✦ The **7th of a 7th chord clashing against the root** – at bar 9¹ the chord is Gm⁷ in first inversion, with the root (G) in the second violin and the 7th (F) in the first violin; the dissonance is resolved as the first violin drops to E and the chord becomes C major on the second beat of the bar.

Corelli sometimes lets the bass move on before there is a resolution of the dissonance, as in bar 7. And he often engineers chains of suspensions in which each resolution prepares the way for the next suspension, as in bars 9–12.

Notice that the figuring of Example 7.11 is slightly different to the system described earlier in this chapter. In particular, horizontal lines are not used, but short notes which don't require a change of harmony, such as the B♭ at the end of bar 1, are usually easy to identify.

When you come to do exercises based on trio sonatas try this working method:

1 Identify key(s) and cadence points.

2 Note any repetitions or sequences.

3 Make outlines for the two added parts. Begin by identifying where dissonances are required by the figuring – often there are many. Then write each dissonant pitch as a notehead, not a precise note value, into one of the violin parts. Often the violin which is currently *lower* in pitch takes the dissonant note. Remember to **prepare and resolve each dissonance in the same part**. For example, if you were completing bars 5–6 of Example 7.11, your Violin II outline might look like this – notice how each resolution (R) also serves as the preparation (P) for the next dissonance in this chain of suspensions):

4 Complete both violin parts by building on and elaborating your outline.

5 Make sure that you have no forbidden consecutives – check the two violin parts against each other as well as checking each violin part with the bass. Also check that the figuring has been correctly observed and not contradicted anywhere, and that all dissonances have been correctly prepared and resolved.

When working on steps 3 and 4, remember that the two violins in a trio sonata are often a 3rd apart – or a 2nd and then a 3rd apart when suspensions are involved. But at the end of sections, the final chord of a perfect cadence often has the violins in unison, two octaves above the bass. This means that both the 3rd and 5th are omitted, as in bars 4, 8 and 12 *below*.

Elsewhere, $\frac{5}{3}$ chords are either complete or have a doubled root and no 5th. Sometimes the ornamental resolution of a suspension completes a chord which would otherwise be incomplete, as in bar 6 *below*, where the second violin jumps down to the 5th of the chord before resolving each 9th.

Ex. 7.11   **Grave**   Corelli: Trio Sonata Op 3 no 1

Your teacher will be able to supply you with suitable practice exercises, based on the simpler movements from Corelli's trio sonatas.

7.12 Two-part baroque counterpoint for keyboard (OCR)

This section is for those studying the baroque counterpoint option in OCR A2 Music. This is a coursework task based on keyboard music in which you have to present a number of worked exercises in which you have added a part to a given part. Although the style is similar in many ways to the two-part music encountered in most of this chapter, figured bass is not involved.

Your teacher will set suitable exercises, in which both parts are given in full at the start, to indicate the style. These may consist of extracts in which both parts have similar melodic interest, or those in which the right hand has the melody and the left provides a mainly supportive role.

Two equal parts

Bach's two-part inventions are works in which both parts share the melodic interest. They were originally played on keyboard instruments of modest range – the lowest note is B, two leger lines below the bass stave, and the highest is C, two leger lines above the treble stave. The two parts do not cross.

Each of Bach's inventions is essentially a working-out of a small number of melodic ideas heard at the beginning. Bach's principal methods of development are

+ Imitation

+ Melodic inversion (where a single part is turned upside down by reversing the direction of its intervals)

+ Contrapuntal inversion (where the whole texture is inverted, the higher part becoming the lower or *vice versa*)

+ Sequence.

Study and play the following passage and then follow the method for working this type of exercise described *below*.

Ex. 7.12.1

Bach: Two-part Invention No 1

1 Identify key(s) and obvious cadence points

The music begins in C major. F#s are in regular use from bar 4 onwards, suggesting G major, and the melodic pattern in bars 6^4–7^1 offers a likely place for a Ic–V–I cadence in that key. F♮ in bar 9 heralds a return to C major at the end of the extract.

2   Identify the principal melodic material and how it is used

The first seven semiquavers of the melody form a motif which is **imitated** by the bass in the same bar. The melody (and almost certainly the bass) of bar 1 is repeated in **sequence** a 5th higher in bar 2. The opening motif is then used in **inversion** in bar 3 (marked with a bracket) and this version is spun out in descending sequence to fill the rest of bars 3 and 4 – it also returns in bars 5 and 6, but this time only the last four semiquavers (marked with a pecked bracket) are used sequentially.

The melody from bars 1–2 returns in the bass of bars 7–8, transposed to G major, and the seven-semiquaver motif appears once more, in inversion, in bar 9.

3   Sketch in an outline of your added parts

Do this by putting in pitches and/or rhythms wherever they seem obvious, using the information gleaned in steps 1 and 2.

The melodic sequence in bar 2 gives the clue for completing the bass in this bar – it also follows in sequence, repeating the imitative entry of bar 1.

When the bass introduced the motif in bar 1 it was accompanied by quavers in the melody, which helped to give each part rhythmic independence. We can use quavers in the bass of bars 3–4, to accompany the continuous semiquavers, although pitches will have to be chosen to harmonise the melody (in 3rds and 6ths).

Compare bars 7–8 with bars 1–2. Do you see that contrapuntal inversion might work in bars 7–8 if the melody imitates the lead taken by the bass?

4   Complete your added parts and check your work

Example 7.12.2 shows the passage after adding the points in step 3 and filling in the remainder of the missing parts – using semiquavers when the melody has quavers or rests, and quavers where it has semiquavers. Finally, check your work, looking out for any forbidden consecutives and ensuring that accidentals are correct.

The working below is grammatically correct but compare it with Bach's original to see how he derived nearly every note from the material in bar 1.

Ex. 7.12.2

Complete the missing parts in the following passage. There are plenty of sequences to help you here. The trill in bars 19–21 must be accompanied by some purposeful semiquaver movement in the left hand.

Bach: Two-part Invention No 4

Melody-dominated keyboard music

In much two-part keyboard music of the late baroque period, the right hand has the dominant part and the left acts as a harmonic support or accompaniment. The style is often not very different from the two-part writing discussed in Section **7.9**, starting on page 109, apart from the fact that the bass is not figured. You may find it helpful to read that section, and to use the exercises (a) and (c) in Activity **7.9** for additional practice – just ignore the figuring in the given bass parts.

The method for working such tests is similar to that described earlier. First identify the key(s) and cadence points, then write an outline of the missing parts by sketching in the most obvious pitches and/or rhythms. Next complete the parts by adding to and elaborating this outline, and finally check your work.

Here is part of a keyboard movement by Bach. Study it and play it.

Ex. 7.12.3
Menuett

Bach: French Suite No 2

Step 1 This a minuet and, like many dances, it consists of mainly four-bar phrases. How do we know? Well, the first clue is that the passage is 24 bars long (6 × 4). The second is that long notes in bars 8, 16 and 24 suggest phrase endings. The third is that between these eight-bar sections, bars 3–4 will support an imperfect cadence in the tonic and bars 11–12 will support a perfect cadence in the relative major. There is no obvious cadence in bars 19–20, so the last eight bars will form one long phrase.

Armed with this information, look closely at the given material and then work out the keys (the subdominant is also visited) and the types of cadence that will fit.

Step 2 The given material suggests that the bass has quaver movement when the melody is not in quavers, but at other times crotchets and occasional rests will be appropriate. The melody, though, has much continuous quaver movement.

There is a clear use of sequence, especially towards the end, and bar 9 should be easy to complete since it seems to be a transposition of bar 1.

Given all this deduction, it should now be possible to dot in at least the first note of most incomplete bars, remembering that 3rds or 6ths between treble and bass are likely to work well. Add roman numerals to show which chords you have identified.

Step 3 Decide whether each group of six quavers in the melody belongs to one chord or to more than one, and identify which notes are non-chord notes. For instance, the first four notes of bar 18 outline V^7 in E♭ major. Perhaps the fifth note (G) is the resolution of that chord, implying chord I? If so, it may be difficult to decide how to make bar 19 sound harmonically fresh, since that seems to imply chord I. In fact, Bach treats the G as an accented passing note and the following F as a harmony note, so that the whole of bar 18 uses dominant harmony and the whole of bar 19 uses the tonic chord, with the C on the third beat treated as an appoggiatura. At this quite late stage in the draft working you should have something like Example 7.12.4, in which there is relatively little left to complete.

Step 4 Try completing the remaining notes yourself – check your working and, if you have access to a copy of Bach's French suites, compare it with the original.

Activity 7.12.2

Complete the missing parts in each of the following pieces in an appropriate style.

(a) This is a little shorter than the 16–24 bars normally expected and only the bass needs completion. The bass pattern in bar 1 returns in one other bar, but elsewhere the bass can use either the rhythm shown in bar 3 or just crotchets and minims.

128 Baroque counterpoint

(b) This piece is in the style of a bourrée (a baroque dance) and is of the length you should expect to submit for your exercises. The given bass part is all in crotchets – it would be possible to use this type of 'walking bass' for the entire bass part.

[**Alla bourrée**]   Handel: HWV 491

8 Middle eights in 32-bar pop songs

8.1 The middle eight

The choruses of many popular songs follow a type of 32-bar structure which has four eight-bar sections in the pattern AABA. **Middle eight** is the name often given to the contrasting B section. You may also see it called the bridge or the release.

This simple but effective structure was often used by popular songwriters in the first half of the 20th century and was adopted by jazz musicians. It has remained in favour ever since, being used by the Beatles, Oasis and many others.

In practice, the form is often given more variety – the sections may be four or 16 bars long rather than eight, there may be more than one bridge, and phrases are sometimes extended so that, for example, the final A section might be ten bars long. But the 32-bar chorus (or song) set by Edexcel for the AS and A2 Music exams keeps to the basic form of eight-bar sections and follows this pattern:

A Eight bars of bass part with chord symbols that finish with two bars (numbered 7a and 8a) marked as a 'first time ending'. A repeat sign directs that …

A is played again, but now the 'first time ending' is skipped and instead the 'second time ending' (bars 7b and 8b) is played instead.

B bars 9–16 form the middle eight, the last two bars of which (bars 15–16) are called the **turnaround** because they prepare the way for a return to the opening material, signified by the instruction *D.C. al Fine* at the end. This is an abbreviation for the Italian *Da Capo al Fine*, meaning go 'from the top to the finish'.

A the first eight bars are played once more, ending at the word *Fine* – this is merely the end of the chorus and so usually finishes on $V^{(7)}$ to prepare the way for a following verse that is not printed.

You are required to write a bass part for the 'second-time ending' plus the whole of the middle eight, ending with a turnaround.

In the Edexcel AS exam you are given the chord symbols for each bar to add, but at A2 you must plan your own harmonies (although there is often a requirement to use a particular chord at a specified place in the middle eight).

Exam tests are not taken from established repertoire. The given material, which often includes more different chords than are found in many songs, is specially composed and not related to the style of any particular songwriter. Each exercise tests two basic compositional techniques – how chords and chord symbols work, and how you can build a bass part, with some melodic and rhythmic interest, from them.

8.2 Chord symbols

The harmonies in popular songs are commonly indicated by chord symbols from which the accompanying players build their individual parts. These are explained in Section **2.5** (page 23) and **2.11** (page 27), which you should revise now. All work in this chapter uses a bass stave and so, if necessary, you should also revise the information about the bass stave given on page 5.

Here is a summary of the symbols you are likely to come across – the last two types in this list are more likely to occur at A2 than at AS.

✦ A note name by itself means a major triad on that note:
G = G major (G B D)   **B♭** = B♭ major (B♭ D F)

✦ A note name followed by **m** means a minor triad on that note:
Gm = G minor (G B♭ D)   **F♯m** = F♯ minor (F♯ A C♯)

✦ A note name followed by **dim** means a diminished triad on that note (i.e. a minor triad but with a diminished 5th):
Gdim = G diminished (G B♭ D♭)   **C♯dim** = C♯ diminished (C♯ E G)

✦ A note name followed by ^{7} means a major triad plus a minor 7th:
G^7 = G 7th (G B D F)   **E♭**^{7} = E♭ 7th (E♭ G B♭ D♭)

✦ A note name followed by **m**^{7} means a minor triad plus a minor 7th:
Gm^7 = G minor 7th (G B♭ D F)   **F♯m**^{7} = F♯ minor 7th (F♯ A C♯ E)

✦ A note name followed by ^{maj7} means a major triad with a major 7th:
G^{maj7} = G with a major 7th (G B D F♯)   **E**^{maj7} = E with a major 7th (E G♯ B D♯)

✦ A note name followed by **dim**^{7} means a diminished 7th chord:
Edim^7 = E diminished 7th (E G B♭ D♭)   **Bdim**^{7} = B diminished 7th (B D F A♭)

✦ A note name followed by **m**$^{7♭5}$ or **m**$^{7♮5}$ means a half-diminished 7th chord: (i.e. a diminished triad with a minor 7th):
Em$^{7♭5}$ = E half-diminished 7th (E G B♭ D)
Bm$^{7♮5}$ = B half-diminished 7th (B D F A) – note that the natural sign is required in this example because Bm means B D F♯, whereas we need B D F♮ A.

The types of chord symbol shown *above* have been used in Edexcel tests, but in other books and music you may find some chords labelled slightly differently. For example, minor chords are sometimes indicated by the abbreviation 'min' rather than just 'm', and other symbols may be used, such as ^{o} for a diminished chord, ^{ø} to indicate a half-diminished 7th, or ^{Δ} for a major 7th chord.

There are several important points to note about chord symbols:

✦ Chord symbols do *not* take account of the key signature (if there is one). So, if there is a B♭ in the key signature, the chord symbol **G** does *not* mean G B♭ D – it means G B D. You would have to write **Gm** if you wanted G B♭ D.

✦ The numeral ^{7} after a letter name, and with no other symbol, always indicates a *minor* 7th above the letter name. So **C**^{7} means C E G B♭, not C E G B♮.

✦ Chord symbols indicate root-position chords, and so the printed letter name is the root of the chord (and thus the main bass note), except …

Slash chords

When the chord symbol is followed by a forward slash and then the name of another note, that second note is the actual bass note. Often this means that the chord is inverted (although slash chords are also used in other circumstances, such as when there is a pedal note in the bass, with different chords above it). So,

✦ **G/B** = a chord of G, with B in the bass (B D G – a first-inversion chord)

✦ **Cm/G** = a chord of C minor, with G in the bass (G C E♭ – a second inversion)

✦ **Gm**^{7}**/F** = a G-minor 7th chord, with F in the bass (F G B♭ D – a third inversion)

✦ **F♯**^{dim7}**/A** = a diminished 7th on F♯, with A in the bass (A C E♭ F♯).

(a) For each symbol below, show the kind of chord required and the letter names of all the notes. For example, $\mathbf{D^7}$ = a D 7th chord (D F♯ A C). Play each chord.

F	**Fm**	**Fdim**	**F/A**	**F**^{7}	**Fm**^{7}	**F**$^{\mathbf{maj7}}$
E	**E♭**	**Bm**	**C♯m**	**Adim**	**F♯dim**	**D/F♯**
Dm/F	**B♭/F**	**B**^{7}	**A♭**^{7}	**Am7**	**B♭m**^{7}	**C**$^{\mathbf{maj7}}$

8.3 The AS middle–eight test

Example 8.3.1 shows the type of test you should expect in the AS examination. The task is to complete the bass part in accordance with the chord symbols. You should aim for some rhythmic variety in your addition, and you should introduce new ideas as well as building on the given material. You are also required to name a suitable instrument, add a tempo indication and suggest a stylistic feel for the piece.

Ex: 8.3.1

Here is a working method for this type of test. Always begin by studying and playing the given material.

Step 1 **Select an instrument, tempo and stylistic feel**

The obvious instrument for the bass part of a popular song is a **bass guitar**, although you may write for double bass if you think this is appropriate. Both instruments normally have four strings tuned to the notes shown *left*. Notice that the bottom note is E, just below the bass stave. At the other end of the range, most players are comfortable at least up to the G on the third leger line above the bass stave. Music for the bass guitar and the double bass sounds an octave lower than notated.

Ex: 8.3.2

Some bass guitars have a fifth string, tuned to B, a fourth lower than the E string, and some double basses have an extension to take the range down to C below the bass stave. If you write for one of these instruments, you must make this clear by stating that the instrument is 'five-string bass' or 'double bass with C extension'. Otherwise, you merely need to state 'bass guitar' or 'double bass'. The latter is usually played *pizzicato* (plucked) in popular music.

Notice that the strings of the bass guitar (like those of the double bass) are tuned in perfect 4ths. This means that the melodic interval of a perfect 4th can easily be played on adjacent strings, and so this interval frequently features in popular-style bass parts – as you can see in the given material *opposite*.

You must indicate the **tempo** (speed) at the head of each exercise. In popular music this is often expressed in beats per minute. For example, 90 bpm (or ♩=90) means 90 beats per minute. However, the tests often have a minim beat, as shown by the ¢ time signature in Example 8.3.1. 90 minims per minute would be very fast for this piece (it is the same as 180 crotchets per minute – three every second!). A more realistic tempo for this exercise might be 60 bpm (or ♩=60).

You can use English words or phrases to indicate tempo as well as (or instead of) a speed in beats per minute. Italian expressions such as *Allegro ma non troppo* are not often used in popular music.

Choose a tempo that you think suits the given material and matches the stylistic feel that you choose – it must be playable at the speed you indicate, and must not sound rushed or unnaturally slow.

It is a good idea to decide on the **stylistic feel** from the outset, so that you can keep this in mind as you add your bass part. It could be a genre or sub-genre of popular music such as rhythm and blues, reggae, or heavy rock. However, you could instead describe the character of the music in broader terms, such as 'with energy', 'light bounce' or 'straight eights' (i.e. the quavers should not be swung). For Example 8.3.1 we'll use the expression 'Relaxed, but with a firm beat'.

Step 2   Add a single note for each chord symbol

Write one note in the bass part where each new chord symbol begins to provide a melodic outline on which you can later build your complete answer. This should be the note whose name appears at the beginning of each chord symbol, except in the case of slash chords, where it must be the note named *after* the forward slash. For instance, you should write F♯ under the symbol **D/F♯** on the second beat of bar 14. Write each note in whichever octave seems most suitable in relation to the notes in neighbouring bars – you may want to change the octave of some notes later.

In some music you may see a freer approach to bass parts. For example, the first (or only) bass in a chord of F might be A, the 3rd of the chord. But in examination work, it is best to interpret the chord symbols strictly, in the manner explained *above*.

Although chord symbols are not key-specific, it is important to have a clear idea of the key you are in, and where the chord progressions are leading. Many chord patterns will be familiar from your study of Chapter 3. For instance, a circle of 5ths starts in bar 7b of this example. The last chord of the turnaround is nearly always V or V^7 – in Example 8.3.1 this is G^7 (leading back to C in bar 1) and, as is often the case, it is approached from the chord a 5th above, D^7. This is one of the secondary 7ths we learnt about in Section **3.18** (page 47). Here is our outline at the end of Step 2:

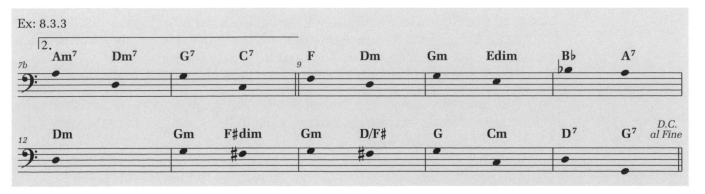

Step 3   **Complete the bass part from this outline**

We must now introduce interesting rhythmic and melodic detail in keeping with the given material, which has two or three notes on each minim beat, except in bars 4 and 8a, where minims give weight to the phrase ends.

To introduce this sort of detail, you can do one or more of the following things, all of which are illustrated in Example 8.3.4 *below*:

✦ Repeat the bass note, either at the same pitch, as in example *(a)*, or in a different octave if the instrument's range allows, as in *(b)*.

✦ Use other notes from the chord, as in example *(c)* – but don't let them become too prominent otherwise you risk changing the nature of the chord. For instance, the pattern in (d) sounds more like **F/C** than a plain chord of **F**.

✦ Include passing notes and/or auxiliary notes, as in example *(e)*.

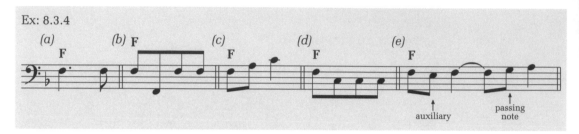

It is not necessary to use every note from the chord, and in the case of 7th chords, the 7th itself is often not played in the bass. For example, look at the second half of bar 1 in Example 8.3.1 on page 132 – the chord is C^7 but the 7th (B♭) does not appear in the bass part.

When the 7th *is* used in the bass part, it is sometimes treated more freely than a 7th in traditional harmony, but it often does resolve down a step if the following chord includes its note of resolution. A 7th often follows other notes of the same chord, perhaps as part of a broken chord, and need not be prepared. In the next example, neither the B♭ in bar 1 nor the E♭ in bar 2 is prepared. You could think of the B♭ resolving to A in bar 2, but the E♭ cannot resolve in the traditional manner because there isn't a D in bar 3.

Now let's look at the detail of how each bar in our outline can be filled out. As you read this, refer to the completed working at the bottom of the next page.

Bars 7b–8b (the second-time bars) begin with the same chords as the first-time bars (7a–8a). So there's no need to go for a different bass pattern in this test – it will work well to repeat the same bass up to the beginning of bar 8b.

Bars 9–10. Bar 10 is a thinly-disguised harmonic sequence of bar 9, one step higher, so it would be good to use a melodic sequence in bars 9–10. In other words, bar 10 can repeat bar 9, one step higher. The final B♭ anticipates the starting note of bar 11 and ensures that the music has already gone a little higher than in the given bars.

Notice the quaver rests and new broken-chord shapes – new ideas are welcome in the middle eight. The second quaver of bar 9 is an auxiliary note between the two Fs, but it also leads the part down towards the D of Dm^7. In the sequence of bar 10 the corresponding auxiliary note is F♯ – again a semitone below the chord notes on either side of it, but this time chromatic. Try an F♮ instead – which do you prefer?

Bars 11–12. Bar 12 is a phrase ending, halfway through the middle eight, and needs only one chord. We've borrowed this from bar 4 (another phrase ending) since a few references back to the given bars are a good thing. Notice that bar 11[1] doesn't have the same rhythm as bars 9[1] and 10[1] (although the melodic shape is the same). Repeating the rhythm exactly in successive bars might be wearisome, especially since it can be used effectively in bar 13 at the start of the next four-bar phrase.

Bars 13–14 have been derived from bars 9–10, to help unify the middle eight. But to add interest, the auxiliary note A in bar 13 now *rises*. In bar 14 it is replaced by an additional harmony note (B♭) which helps the melodic line to expand. Bar 14 is similar harmonically to bar 13, but we've built on the slight difference by taking the bass up to a high D in bar 14.

Bars 15–16. Each bar has chords whose roots fall a 5th, and it is possible again to use sequence. However, to create a good melodic line, our original bass notes (shown in lighter type *below*) have been shifted to a different octave. There is another octave shift in bar 7b, for the same reason. At the end of the middle eight, bar 16 leads back smoothly to bar 1 – just what is wanted at this point.

Step 4   **Check everything for accuracy, and for rhythmic and melodic interest**

Make sure that you have indicated the instrument, tempo and stylistic feel at the start. Then check that all bars have been completed (especially the two second-time bars) and that they have the correct number of beats. Ensure that your added part doesn't contradict the chord symbols, and that it doesn't go beyond the range of the chosen instrument. Remember to take special care over accidentals. For instance, in bar 14 below the chord of G minor needs a B♭, while in bar 16 the chord of D[7] needs F♯.

Check that your added part includes some interesting new ideas as well as some that build on the given material. If you choose to submit your work as a computer printout, note that you *must* include the given material (without any alterations) and all of the chord symbols throughout the piece.

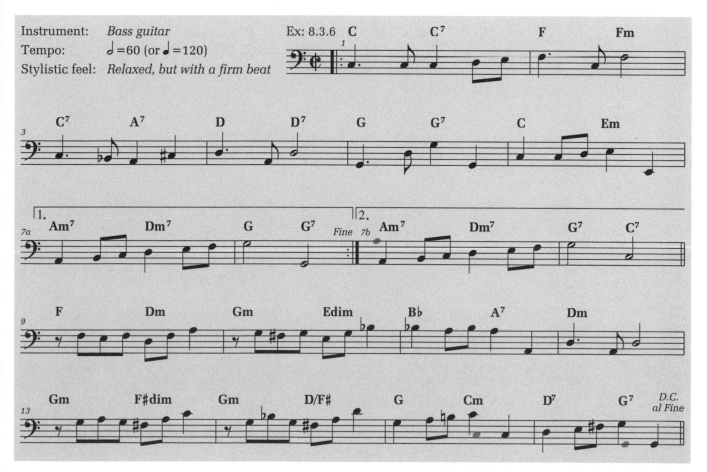

(a) The following is another working of the last ten bars of Example 8.3.1 – and it is far from successful! Identify all the mistakes and misjudgements, including any wrong notes and missing accidentals.

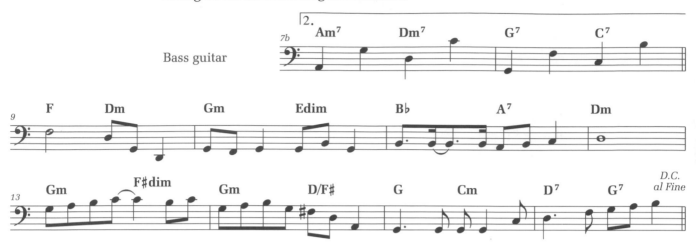

(b) In each of the following bars, write two crotchets that will both fit the given chord symbols. The first answer is given.

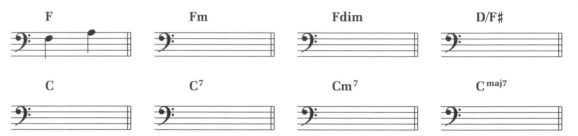

(c) In each of the following bars, write two quavers and a crotchet to fit the given chord symbols. The first two answers are given. The second quaver can be either an additional harmony note, as in the first answer, or a passing note, as in the second answer.

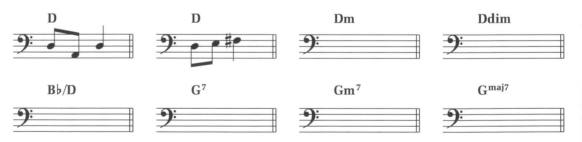

Re-read chapter 4 if you are unsure about these types of melodic decoration.

(d) Label each note marked with an arrow *below* as one of the following:

ANT (anticipation)   APN (accented passing note)   AUX (auxiliary note)
CPN (chromatic passing note)   HN (harmony note)   PN (passing note)

8.4 Hints and tips for good bass parts

Read Section **5.3** on melody writing (pages 64–65) and note the following additional points about completing bass parts:

✦ Bass parts generally have more **leaps** than melodies, particularly between notes of the current chord, but use melodic decoration such as passing notes in order to obtain some contrasting **stepwise movement**. Balance ascending and descending patterns, and try to get well-judged points of climax and relaxation.

✦ Aim to cover at least as wide a **range** as the given material and try to go higher at some point in order to give the middle eight a lift. If you need to extend the range of a narrow outline, consider moving some notes up or down an octave.

✦ Make sure that your bass has a **clear phrase structure**. Middle eights often have two four-bar phrases, and these may sometimes divide into two-bar pairs.

You can use a longer note to mark phrase ends, such as the minim in (a) *below*, or you can separate phrases with a rest, as in (b). Using a semibreve for an entire bar, as in (c), is less good, as the lack of movement will make the bass too static.

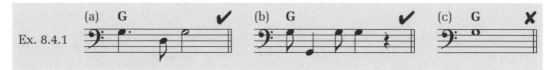

Ex. 8.4.1

Another alternative for the last bar of a phrase is to write a **fill** to lead into the next phrase. The 'bass run' in (a) *below* is a simple scale pattern. A more chromatic fill in shown in (b), while the fill in (c) starts (rather unusually) on a non-chord note. If you do this, be sure to resolve the dissonance onto a harmony note, as here.

Ex. 8.4.2

✦ Look for **repeating patterns**. If the chord symbols imply a harmonic sequence, use them to support a melodic sequence in the bass. If there are straight repeats, use repetition in the bass, perhaps lightly ornamented for greater interest.

Activity 8.4

Write an outline bass part for the following chord symbols. Then choose your own rhythms for this exercise – but assume the speed is quite fast, so don't use notes shorter than a quaver. Check that you have added all necessary accidentals, especially in bars 10 and 15.

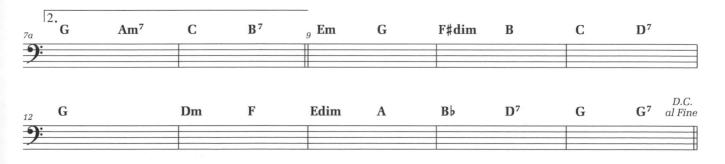

8.5 Practice exercises

Activity 8.5 provides three practice exercises for Edexcel AS middle-eight tests. Study the given material for clues on how to proceed. For instance, (a) includes several distinctive rhythms, any of which might feature, or be developed, in the middle eight. There is a certain amount of chromaticism in (b), including a short chromatic link at the end of bar 8a, while syncopation is a feature in many of the given bars of (c).

In (c) $\frac{4}{4}$ time and the use of semiquaver patterns suggest that the speed should not be too fast. The diagonal-line symbols in bar 14 indicate that the **Ddim** chord lasts for three beats, so the chord of **G** should not appear until the fourth beat of this bar.

<table>
<tr><td style="background:black;color:white;text-align:center">**Activity 8.5**</td></tr>
</table>

Complete the bass part in each of the following, in accordance with the given chord symbols. For each one, indicate your choice of instrument, tempo, and stylistic feel. Aim for some rhythmic variety and introduce new ideas as well as building on the given material.

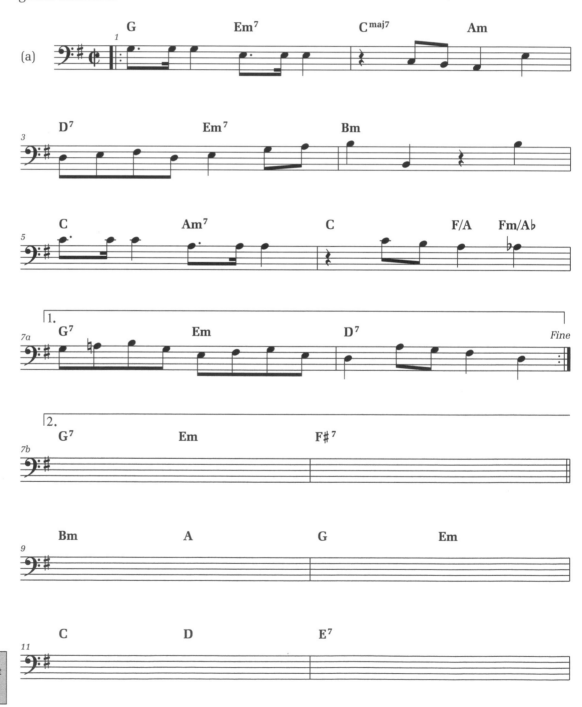

8.6 The A2 middle-eight test

For Edexcel A2 Music the middle-eight test has to be completed under examination conditions rather than as coursework, although you are allowed access to an instrument on which to try out your work. The method for completing the test is similar to that described in Section **8.3**, except that you also have to choose your own key(s) and chords for the bass part that you add:

1   Study and play the given material, then select a suitable instrument, tempo, and (if possible at this stage) stylistic feel

2   Choose keys and chords for bars 7b–16, as explained in the next section, and write in the chord symbols

3   Add a single note for each of your chosen chord symbols

4   Complete the bass part from this outline

5   Check everything for accuracy, and for rhythmic and melodic interest.

8.7 Choosing keys and chords

Example 8.7.1 shows the type of test you should expect at A2:

Choosing keys First you need to identify the key(s) of the given material, because:

✦   Your second-time bars must follow on from the key and chord in bar 6

✦   The key of your middle eight should normally relate to the key of the A section, although it shouldn't be the same

✦   The end of your middle eight needs to lead back effectively to the key of bar 1 in order for the turnaround to work properly.

The first chord in bar 1 is usually the tonic chord. Here it is E minor, and this is confirmed as the main key by the dominant 7th of E minor (**B**^{7}) in bar 8a, which leads straight back to E minor for the repeat. The key of bar 6 is less clear, but it appears to be C major, judging from **G**^{7} (the dominant 7th of C) at the end of the bar, resolving to a chord of C major at the start of bar 7a.

Now look at the chord symbol (**Am**) that lurks almost unnoticed in bar 9. At least one chord symbol is always given somewhere in the middle eight – partly to help you, but also to challenge you to work around this fixed point. Here, the given chord is at the start of the middle eight, for which it could be a suitable key chord – A minor is the subdominant of E minor (the key of the A section), and so would provide contrast with the given key while still being related to it.

If the given chord occurs later in the middle eight there could be more possibilities – for example, **Am** might still be treated as chord I of A minor, but you could instead decide to set the middle eight in G major (the relative major), treating **Am** as chord ii in that key.

The key you choose for the middle eight is best established in bar 9, at the start of the section. This means that your second-time bars must not only provide a smooth transition from bar 6 but must also modulate to the new key. Similarly, the last two bars of the middle eight must modulate back in the direction of the tonic, for the final repeat of the A section.

To avoid too much tonal instability, it is usually best not to include any dramatic modulation within the middle eight itself, although a brief visit to a closely related key (such as the dominant of your chosen key) will often work well at the halfway point in bar 12.

If you enjoy a challenge, by all means experiment with more remote keys for the middle eight (providing the given chord can be incorporated in a logical fashion) but experiments may be wiser during lessons and homework rather than in the exam room! Try, for example, the flat submediant if the starting key is major (F major in an A major piece) or the flat supertonic in a minor key (B♭ major in an A minor piece).

When you come to Steps 3–4 it is possible that the key(s) you have chosen turn out to be less suitable than you had hoped – in which case, don't be afraid to reconsider.

Choosing chords

Aim to have two chords in most bars as too many single-chord bars will limit the scope of your work. The possible exceptions are the phrase endings in bars 8b, 12 and 16, where a single chord followed by a short rest (like the one given in bar 8a in Example 8.7.1), or elaborated with a fill, may help to define the structure.

First tackle the modulation needed in bars 7b–8b. You need to arrive on the tonic chord of A minor at the start of bar 9. Since the most effective way of modulating is by means of the progression V^7–I, use V^7 of A minor (which is E^7) in bar 8b.

See Section **6.9** on pages 78–80 if you are unsure about cadence approach chords.

Now you need a good approach chord for this perfect cadence, but first remember that a chord of **C** will work well at the *start* of bar 7b (as it does in bar 7a) in order to resolve the G^7 at the end of bar 6. The approach chord should therefore go in the second half of bar 7b, where it can also act as a pivot between C major and A minor.

There are several possibilities, but ii^7b (one of the most common of all approach chords) would work particularly well. In A minor this is $Bm^{7♭5}/D$ and it is a good choice because it is both vii^7b in C major (the key we are leaving) and ii^7b in A minor (the key we are approaching) – it is a pivot chord. The chords for the second-time bars are now complete, along with the first (given) chord of bar 8:

$$|C \quad Bm^{7♭5}/D \quad | E^7 \quad\quad || Am$$

Next, look at bars 15–16, in which the music should normally end on $V^{(7)}$ of the key used in bar 1 – so $B^{(7)}$ is needed in this particular exercise. You could use this chord throughout the bar, or V in the first half and V^7 in the second. Another possibility is to use a cadence approach chord at the start of bar 16, thus delaying the dominant chord until later in the bar. Whatever you choose, you will need an approach chord for $V^{(7)}$, either at the start of bar 16 or in the second half of bar 15.

Next turn your attention to bar 12, which is the end of the first phrase in the middle eight. If you have decided not to modulate, this would be a good place to arrive on the dominant chord. Our middle eight is in A minor, so that would mean a chord of **E** (major) in bar 12 – also choose an appropriate approach chord to go in the second half of bar 11 in order to form a cadence. To provide some chromatic interest, and show your skill, you could choose $V^{(7)}$ of V – $\mathbf{B^{(7)}}$ in the key of A minor.

Alternatively, you may prefer to use two different keys in your middle eight – perhaps A minor in bars 9–12 and then G major. In this case it would be preferable to end the first half on V of the new key (**D** at the end of bar 12) to be followed by I of the new key (**G**) in bar 13.

Now draft the rest of your chord scheme, playing and evaluating everything as you go along. Don't be afraid to choose quite basic progressions of the sort discussed in Chapter 4, such as roots that fall in 3rds or fragments of the circle of 5ths. The most important thing is that your progressions must sound as if they are leading towards the keys and chords you have already decided upon for bars 12 and 16.

The kinds of chords described in Chapter 3 are fine for completing middle eights – major, minor and diminished triads, and 7ths, with their inversions. For more colour you might include a secondary dominant or half-diminished 7th. If you know how to use other types of chord (augmented triads, added 6ths, sus chords or 9ths) then you are free to use them, but it is better to aim for strong, simple progressions than to attempt to dazzle with complex chords that don't fulfil any real musical purpose.

Elaborating simple chord patterns

Once the basic chord scheme is settled, how can you make it more interesting? Much depends on context and experiment, but one or more of the following 'tricks of the trade' should work with most progressions:

✦ **Using 7th chords** in place of plain triads. Try playing **Dm Gm Edim A Dm**, and then compare the difference when you play $\mathbf{Dm^7\ Gm^7\ Edim^7\ A^7\ Dm}$.

✦ **Using inversions** ('slash chords') will provide variety and will also often help the bass line to flow.

✦ Using **secondary dominants** can spice up (and extend) stock progressions – try playing $\mathbf{C\ Am\ Dm\ G^7\ C}$, and then play it again with secondary dominants before the second and third chords: $\mathbf{C\ E^7\ Am\ A^7\ Dm\ G^7\ C}$. Further examples are given on the next page.

✦ A **chromatic progression** can be effective, providing there is harmonic stability on either side of it. For instance, look at staves (c) and (d) in Example 8.7.2 on the next page, and bars 3–6 in Activity 8.8 (c) on page 147. Such progressions should not be over-used – if in doubt leave them out!

✦ **Chord substitutions** can work well. The simplest is to 'borrow' the minor version of chord IV when the major version is expected. Play **C F G C** and then compare it with **C Fm G C**. A more advanced technique is to use a 'tritone substitution' chord – that is, to replace one of the chords in a simple progression with a chord an augmented 4th or diminished 5th lower – for example, F^7 in place of B^7).

✦ **Varying the rate of harmonic change** (the frequency with which chords change). Changing the chord on every minim beat can become too predictable. Sometimes it may sound better if you change chord on the last crotchet of a bar, for example: $\mathbf{|\ Dm\ /\ /\ G^7/B\ |\ C}$.

✦ **Increasing the rate of harmonic change immediately before a cadence** will provide variety and clarify the phrasing. This is usually done by inserting a third chord in the penultimate bar of the phrase, and then relaxing the tension by having no change of chord in the last bar of the phrase: $\mathbf{|\ Am\ /\ Dm\ G^7\ |\ C}$.

Simple chord patterns such as I–vi–ii–V–I (and those discussed *below*) can be very useful at the end of the middle eight where, by simply omitting the final tonic chord, they can provide the foundation for the turnaround and its approach. However, if you decide to use such a standard progression, then in an A2 exam you should show that you can elaborate it and take it a little beyond its basic form.

Example 8.7.2 shows how a familiar chord pattern could be developed. In (a) the progression I–IV–V^7–I is shown in C major. In (b) this progression has been extended by two secondary dominants, marked *. By inverting the secondary dominants, a strong chromatic ascent can be achieved in the bass, as shown in (c). Sometimes diminished triads or diminished 7ths can be substituted for secondary dominants. They will have roots a major 3rd higher than the secondary dominants they replace, as shown in (d).

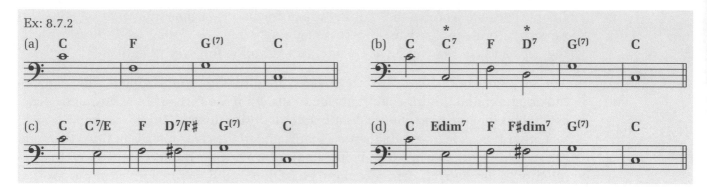

Let's consider one more standard chord pattern, I–vi–IV–ii–V–I (the 'falling 3rds' progression from Section **3.14**). In the key of G major it is **G Em C Am D G**.

✦ By adding secondary dominants before each of the four middle chords this could be extended as far as **G B⁷ Em G⁷ C E⁷ Am A⁷ D⁽⁷⁾ G**. Obviously you can use fewer than four secondary dominants here!

✦ By using some tritone substitution, major–minor substitution, and by adding 7ths, we might arrive at something like this: **G F⁷ E⁷ D♭⁷ C⁷** … and so on.

Activity 8.7

(a) Extend and elaborate each of the following progressions:
In the key of F major: **F Gm C Dm B♭ C F**
In the key of D minor: **Dm A B♭ F Gm Edim A Dm**

(b) Following the advice given in Section 8.7, complete the chords and an outline bass part for Example 8.7.1 (page 141). Remember that the middle eight begins in A minor – you must decide if you want a different key in the second four-bar phrase before the return to E minor.

Then complete the bass part, using the outline you have created. Consider some use of semiquavers, but check that what you write is feasible at your selected tempo. If possible, include some notes that take the player well above middle C (up to F or G above the stave).

Remember that melodic decoration (perhaps including chromatic passing notes) and additional harmony notes will help in creating musical interest and a sense of flow in the bass part.

Check your final working (as described in Step 4 on page 135) and make sure that you have included the instrument, tempo and stylistic feel at the start.

8.8 Practice exercises

Activity 8.8 provides three practice exercises for Edexcel A2 middle-eight tests. Study the given material for an indication of the overall key, as well as the harmonic and melodic style of the bass part. In (c) the **C** ($\frac{4}{4}$) time signature and frequent use of triplet patterns suggest that the speed should not be too fast.

Add chord symbols and complete the bass part in each of the following. The given chord may last for a whole bar or only for part of it. For each exercise, indicate your choice of instrument, tempo, and stylistic feel. Aim for some rhythmic variety in your bass part and introduce new ideas as well as building on the given material.

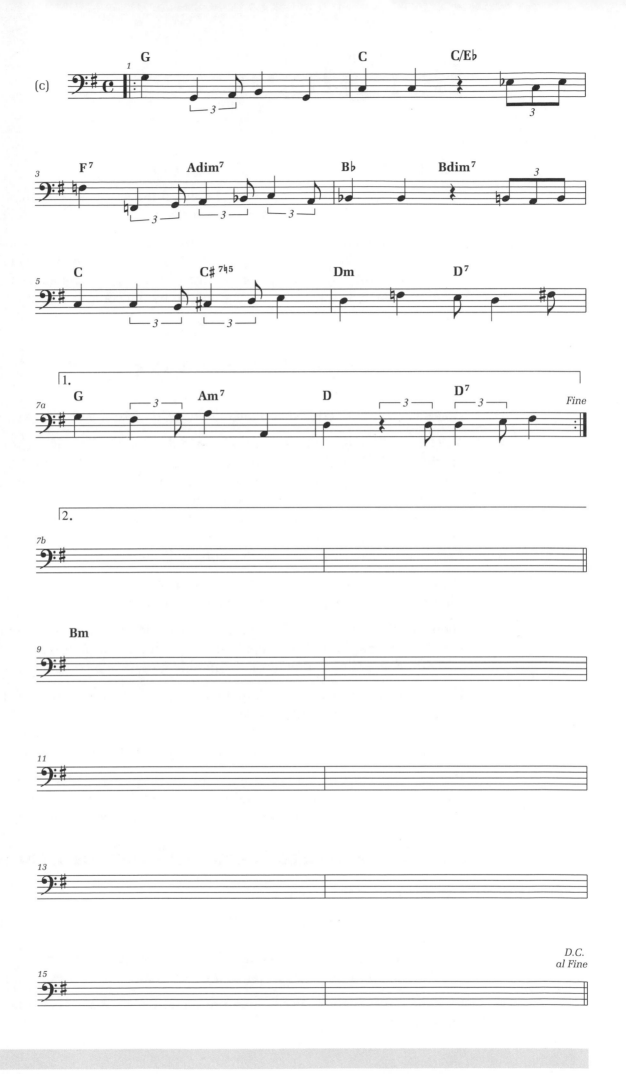

9 Serialism

9.1 Twelve-note serialism and atonality

Serialism is a method of composing based on the systematic use of a fixed series of musical pitches. Sometimes other elements, such as note values, form part of a series.

12-note serialism, the most common form, was developed by Arnold Schoenberg (1874–1951) in the 1920s. Here the series has 12 pitches, and rhythm is not subject to serial control. The series is formed from every note of the chromatic scale, each used only once, in a particular order chosen by the composer. Here is an example of a 12-note series:

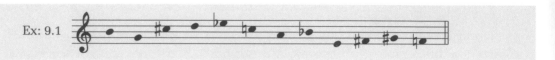

A series is often referred to as a 'note row' or 'tone row' – or even just a 'row'.

Most 12-note music is **atonal**. In other words, there is little if any sense of key. No single note is central – in contrast to tonal music, in which the tonic is heard as the key note. Patterns such as major or minor triads that help build the sense of key in tonal music are avoided or little used in most atonal writing. However, sometimes there are less obvious hints of tonality. In Example 9.1 the notes D E♭ C♮ A B♭ *could* belong to B♭ major, just as the first five notes of this example, and the first four of Example 9.8.2 on page 154, *could* belong to D minor.

Serial music has never been popular. Some people dismiss it as mechanical and even unmusical, but it requires as much skill and judgement as any other type of music.

People don't all use the same terminology when describing serial technique. However, the terms employed in this chapter are very widely accepted and will be recognised by Edexcel examiners. If you use a different system, add an explanatory note.

In this chapter we shall learn how to continue a given opening to make a complete serial melody of about 12 bars, an option for the Edexcel AS Music exam. You are given one complete statement of the series, usually about three bars long, and have to add three or four more statements in a way that fits the style of the given material.

We shall also work on the serialism option for the Edexcel A2 Music exam. Again you are given a melodic passage containing one complete statement of a series, but this time you have to compose a two-part piece lasting for about 20 bars.

Activity 9.1

Listen to some 12-note music, for example:

✦ Schoenberg's *Variations for Orchestra*, Op 31 and String Quartet No 4, Op 37
✦ Berg's *Lyric Suite* (1926)
✦ Webern's Symphony, Op 21 and Quartet, Op 22 (the first movement of the quartet is included in the *Edexcel New Anthology of Music*).

In what ways do these pieces sound different from older classical music? What are the similarities?

9.2 The chromatic scale and use of accidentals

A **chromatic scale** is a succession of semitones, not a mixture of tones and semitones as occurs in major and minor scales. There are 12 different pitches in a chromatic scale (you may find it useful to refer back to the keyboard layout on page 7):

Ex: 9.2.1

C   C#/Db   D   D#/Eb   E   F   F#/Gb   G   G#/Ab   A   A#/Bb   B

Because atonal music is not in a key it never needs a key signature. All sharps and flats are written in as **accidentals**.

With accidentals each sharp or flat lapses after the bar in which it appears. For instance, in Example 9.2.2 *below* the ♯ sign before the F in bar 1 doesn't affect the F in bar 2. However, it may make things clearer to the player if the F in bar 2 is written as F♮ – this is known as a **cautionary accidental**. It is a good idea to include cautionary accidentals if there is any risk of misunderstanding an intended pitch.

Ex: 9.2.2

Some serial composers write a natural sign before every single note that is not a sharp or flat (see Example 9.8.2 on page 154). However, this is not necessary and can make the music look more complicated than it really is.

Double flats and double sharps are avoided in serial music. Unusual accidentals are generally avoided as well, so that F is preferred to E♯, and B is preferred to C♭.

9.3 Versions of the series

In serial music composers don't simply repeat exactly the same arrangement of the 12 pitches of the series over and over again. They use different versions of the chosen series to give variety, while maintaining the identity of the series and the unity of the piece. There are four principal versions of a series, known as

✦ **Prime** – the prime or original order. Usually abbreviated to P, but some people use the letter O (for original) instead

✦ **Inversion** (I) – in which the intervals of P are turned upside down

✦ **Retrograde** (R) – this is P played backwards

✦ **Retrograde inversion** (RI) – this is I played backwards.

Each of the P, I, R and RI versions may be transposed to start on any of the 12 notes of the chromatic scale, so 48 versions of a series are possible in all.

The total number of series available is just over 479 million, a seemingly vast resource! But in practice composers choose the notes of their series, and the versions they use, very carefully in order to achieve the precise musical results they intend.

9.4 Inverting the series

The inversion of a series involves reversing the direction of every interval in the prime order. In I each *rising* interval of P becomes a *falling* interval of the same number of semitones, and each *falling* interval becomes a *rising* interval of the same number of semitones.

We can work out an inversion in terms of major, minor, perfect, diminished and augmented intervals. Example 9.4.1 has the beginning of a series, with its inversion:

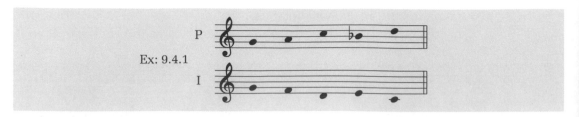

Ex: 9.4.1

Notice that the first note of P becomes the first note of I. The first interval in P is a *rising* major 2nd (G–A), so the first interval of I is a *falling* major 2nd (G–F). The second interval in P is a *rising* minor 3rd (A–C). Therefore the second interval of I is a *falling* minor 3rd (F–D), and so on.

In a moment, we'll look at a different way to invert a series, using the number of semitones in each interval. This can be useful when inverting complicated (diminished or augmented) intervals, and also when there's a choice of note name – for instance, when a note could be written as either C♯ or D♭.

First, how do we decide whether a note should be C♯ or D♭, G♯ or A♭, and so on? At this stage, to avoid possible confusion, **each note name in P must also appear in I**. For example, if there is a C♯ in P, use C♯ not D♭ in I.

To invert the series given in Example 9.1 on page 148, first write in the letter name of each note. Then label the first note 0. Under each of the other notes add a number to indicate how many semitones it is above the starting note. The quickest way is to look through the series for the note a semitone higher than the starting note (C) and label it 1. Then look for C♯ and label it 2, next label D as 3 and so on.

During the numbering, imagine that all notes are *above* the starting note – so A is labelled as 10, even though it is actually two semitones below B:

Ex: 9.4.2

Now for the inversion itself. It begins with the first note (B) of the prime order. For the other notes:

✦ Read the numeral below the second note of P, which is 8.

✦ Subtract this from 12, giving 4.

✦ Find the note in P which has the number 4 – it is E♭. This will be the second note of I. Write it on the top space, a few notes *higher* than B, because the second note of P was a few notes lower than B.

✦ Confirm that the inversion so far is correct. Yes, E♭ is four semitones above B, just as G in the original series is four semitones below B.

Continue in the same way for all the other notes. So, the third note of P is 2. Subtract 2 from 12, giving 10. Find the note in P with the numeral 10, which is A. Write A *below* the previous note in the inversion, because in the original series the third note is *above* the second. Check that A is correct – it is two semitones below the starting note, just as C♯ in the original series was two semitones higher than the starting note.

Continue this process, always subtracting the note number in P from 12 to give the note name for I, until the inversion is finished:

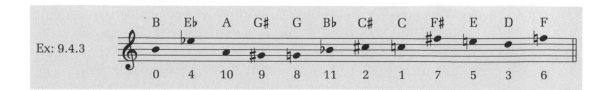

Ex: 9.4.3

B	Eb	A	G#	G	Bb	C#	C	F#	E	D	F
0	4	10	9	8	11	2	1	7	5	3	6

Activity 9.4

On a sheet of manuscript paper, write out an inversion of each of the following three note rows. The first will end on Eb on the bottom line of the stave.

(i)

(ii)

(iii)

9.5 Retrograde, and retrograde inversion

Retrograde means 'backwards'. Here is the series from Example 9.4.2 *opposite*, with its retrograde (R):

Ex: 9.5.1

The retrograde inversion is the inverted version of the row backwards. Here is the I version of the series from Example 9.4.3 *above*, followed by RI:

Ex: 9.5.2

Activity 9.5

Write out the R and RI versions of the three series given in Activity 9.4.

9.6 The magic square

A **magic square** (or matrix) is a diagram which shows all 48 versions of a series – that is, P, I, R and RI, together with all their transposed versions.

There are several ways of setting out a magic square, but the method described below is among the simplest. For convenience, the notes will be shown not as pitches in specific octaves but as **pitch classes**.

There are 12 pitch classes in western music, one for each note of the chromatic scale. The pitch class D, for example, means D in *any* octave. The pitch class F# means F# – or Gb – in *any* octave.

Some internet websites, such as http://www.dancavanagh.com/music/matrix.php, will make magic squares for any series you input. Under present regulations (2006) these sites cannot be accessed during the Edexcel A2 exam. You can use them at other times, but making your own square by hand is valuable in helping you see the characteristic interval properties of a series.

In a magic square, the transpositions of a row are described with subscript numbers. So P_0 means the original version of the series, P_1 means the original row transposed up by a semitone, P_2 is the row transposed up by two semitones and so on. The other versions of the row are similarly referred to as $I_0 \ldots I_{11}$, $R_0 \ldots R_{11}$ and $RI_0 \ldots RI_{11}$.

Here's how to make a magic square. The one *below* is based on the series first shown in Example 9.1 on page 148 – refer to this diagram as you read the instructions. First rule up a sheet of paper with a grid of horizontal and vertical lines like the one below.

◆ Write out P_0 from left to right in the top row of boxes (shown here with a white background). Label it on the left as P_0 and on the right as R_0. It is P_0 when read from left to right, and it gives you R_0 when read from right to left.

◆ Work out I_0, and write it in the first column (shown here with a white background) running down from the first note of P_0. Label the top of the column I_0 and the bottom of the column RI_0. It is I_0 when read from top to bottom, and it gives you RI_0 when read from bottom to top.

◆ You now have the first note for each transposition of P in the first column, and the first note for each transposition of I across the top. Label all P and I versions with subscript numerals according to the number of semitones by which each is higher than the starting note of P_0. For example, the second column is labelled 8 because G is eight semitones higher than B, the next is labelled 2 because C♯ is two semitones higher than B, and so on.

◆ Write in the first note of P_0 repeatedly to form a left-right downward diagonal. This gives you something to check against as you continue to construct your square:

	I_0 ▼	I_8	I_2	I_3	I_4	I_1	I_{10}	I_{11}	I_5	I_7	I_9	I_6	
P_0 ▶	B	G	C♯	D	E♭	C	A	B♭	E	F♯	G♯	F	◀ R_0
P_4	E♭	B	F	F♯	G	E	C♯	D	G♯	B♭	C	A	R_4
P_{10}	A	F	B	C	C♯	B♭	G	G♯	D	E	F♯	E♭	R_{10}
P_9	G♯	E	B♭	B	C	A	F♯	G	C♯	E♭	F	D	R_9
P_8	G	E♭	A	B♭	B	G♯	F	F♯	C	D	E	C♯	R_8
P_{11}	B♭	F♯	C	C♯	D	B	G♯	A	E♭	F	G	E	R_{11}
P_2	C♯	A	E♭	E	F	D	B	C	F♯	G♯	B♭	G	R_2
P_1	C	G♯	D	E♭	E	C♯	B♭	B	F	G	A	F♯	R_1
P_7	F♯	D	G♯	A	B♭	G	E	F	B	C♯	E♭	C	R_7
P_5	E	C	F♯	G	G♯	F	D	E♭	A	B	C♯	B♭	R_5
P_3	D	B♭	E	F	F♯	E♭	C	C♯	G	A	B	G♯	R_3
P_6	F	C♯	G	G♯	A	F♯	E♭	E	B♭	C	D	B	R_6
	▲ RI_0	RI_8	RI_2	RI_3	RI_4	RI_1	RI_{10}	RI_{11}	RI_5	RI_7	RI_9	RI_6	

+ Complete all the horizontal rows (this gives a full set of vertical columns as well). Each horizontal row is a transposition of the top line, P_0 – for example, the second line (labelled P_4) will be higher than the top line (P_0) by four semitones. Use only note names found in P_0 – G♯ not A♭, F♯ not G♭, and so on.

Here is probably the quickest method of working out the transpositions:

  + Find the horizontal row labelled P_1. This will need to contain notes that are each a semitone higher than P_0. For example, P_0 has G as its second note, so P_1 will have G♯; P_0 has C♯ as its third note, so P_1 will have D – and so on. When you have a choice of note names, such as either F♯ or G♭, remember that you must always use the name that appeared somewhere in P_0.

  + Now find the horizontal row labelled P_2 and complete that in a similar way – P_2 is a semitone higher than P_1, and in our example it will begin C♯ A E♭.

  + Continue by adding each of the other horizontal rows in turn – P_3, P_4 and so on – each a semitone higher than the previous one. At some stage you may prefer to start working downwards from P_0 – for example, P_{11} is a semitone below P_0.

It's easy to make mistakes when transposing. However, the position of the first note of the series (B) that you wrote in across the diagonal earlier, will help you check that, as you write in each new transposition, you are still correct. When you've completed several horizontal rows, it is a good idea to pause occasionally and make sure that each new row corresponds with P_0. For example, when you fill in P_4, each note should be four semitones above the corresponding note of P_0. Use the keyboard layout on page 7 to help you do this.

+ Finally, label the R and RI versions.

Summary

You will normally need to select only a few of the 48 possible versions of a series, but a magic square is a good way of seeing the melodic resources available to you. Here is a summary of how the square works:

+ P and its transpositions   … run horizontally … from left to right

+ I and its transpositions   … run vertically   … from top to bottom

+ R and its transpositions   … run horizontally … from right to left

+ RI and its transpositions … run vertically   … from bottom to top

+ The basic untransposed versions of P, I, R and RI have a subscript zero (e.g. P_0)

+ The subscript numerals show how many semitones a transposition is above the original version (for example P_3 is three semitones above P_0)

+ The first note of P_0 is always repeated in the diagonal from top left to bottom right of the square.

Activity 9.6

(a) Copy the series given in Example 9.1 on page 148. Then below it, using the magic square *opposite*, write out the notes of P_4, I_5, R_{10} and RI_6.

(b) Make a magic square for the following series – which you can use again when you get to Section **9.12**: D F B C♯ G E E♭ A A♭ C B♭ F♯.

(c) Referring to the magic square in (b), write out P_1, P_6, I_{11}, R_9 and RI_4.

9.7 Some more basics of serialism

In serial music any note of the series can appear in any reasonable octave. Example 9.7, with all its large leaps, is perfectly possible:

This example illustrates another feature of serial music – the use of very detailed performing directions, emphasising the expressive impact of individual pitches and short groups of notes.

Each new statement of the series must follow on well from the previous one. For instance, it is generally not a good idea to follow P_0 with R_0, since the retrograde version starts on the same pitch as the last note in the prime order. This means that the same pitch would be used twice in succession, giving it undesirable prominence. Sometimes composers make one note serve as both the end of one version of the row and the start of another, to avoid this effect.

In two-part writing, care must also be taken when using using two different versions of the row simultaneously that notes don't coincide in a way which gives unintended prominence to one particular pitch.

Occasionally a note (or small group of notes) may be repeated immediately, as in Example 9.8.1 *below* – but again there is a danger of over-emphasising the pitches concerned, especially if the repeated notes are long. If in doubt, avoid note repetition.

With 12-note serialism, note-values are not governed by the series, but are freely chosen. Example 9.7 *above* has one of thousands, if not millions, of possible rhythms for the series shown in Example 9.1.

9.8 12-note serial melodies: introduction

12-note serial music is not a single, uniform style. For example, some composers, including Schoenberg and Berg, place more emphasis on traditional melodic values than do others such as Webern.

Example 9.8.1 is a melody by Schoenberg. There are strong hints of D minor at the beginning, fairly narrow intervals and conventional rhythms, including repeated

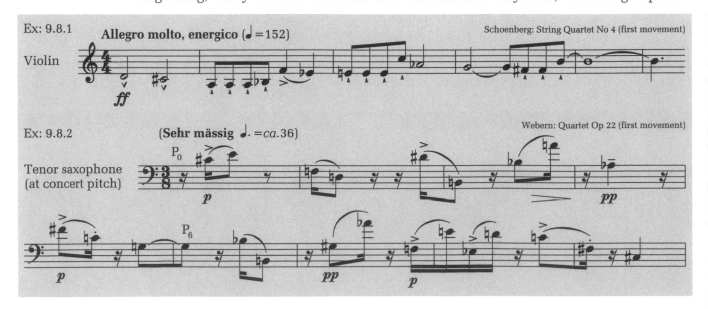

notes. Short motifs, especially the four-quaver pattern, are treated almost as in much classical and Romantic music.

Example 9.8.2 is by Webern and is clearly much more angular and disjointed than Schoenberg's melody. However, repeated use of the opening two-note rhythmic cell provides plenty of coherence and unity.

In some serial music there is extreme diversity, with few or no repeated patterns and motifs. You will probably find it easier to produce effective melodies if you aim for some traditional motivic development, as shown in Examples 9.9 and 9.10 *below*.

We're going to use these two examples, which have been composed specifically for this chapter, as part of our approach to the Edexcel AS serialism option. We can't model our work directly on pieces by established composers, as with chorales and baroque counterpoint, because composers of serial music haven't in general written the kind of self-contained 12-bar melodies that we need.

It is very useful to hear, play and study as much serial music as you can, but you don't have to demonstrate a detailed knowledge of any particular composer's style in the serialism option for either AS or A2 Music.

9.9 12-note serial melodies (i)

Melodic characteristics

Example 9.9 is based on the note row in Example 9.1. It is a simple working, with no complicated rhythms or leaps larger than the augmented octave in bar 10.

Successful serial melodies, like any others, have the following characteristics:

✦ **A clear phrase structure**

It is easy to hear where phrases begin and end in this example, partly because of the detailed performance instructions. Each of the four phrases corresponds to a statement of the series – but remember that phrases and statements of the series don't have to correspond, nor do you have to write four phrases in a serial melody.

✦ **A satisfying overall structure (form)**

You may hear this as binary form (two balanced sections divided by the rest in bar 7) – or perhaps as an AA^1BA^2 structure, achieved largely through rhythm. Phrases one, two and four feature a ♩. ♪ ♩ ♩ pattern. The third phrase offers contrast by being a little more active rhythmically. The melody does *not* use ABA ternary form. In a 12-bar piece, simple ternary with its extended repetition of A is too limiting. Try to show more variety in the nine or ten bars that you add.

Example 9.9 also takes you on a clear emotional journey:

♦ The given first phrase is fairly calm.

♦ The second phrase is bolder, with its climactic top B♭, wider range, greater use of leaps, and more powerful dynamics – but it has lost almost all its energy by the end (*mesto* is Italian for sorrowful or melancholy).

♦ The third phrase recovers – but although more assertive it doesn't go as high, and its intervals are relatively narrow. However, it leads straight into …

♦ The final climactic final phrase – bar 10 has the highest note of all (B♮), the greatest number of large intervals and the most powerful dynamics. The phrase relaxes towards the end, finishing with a calmly optimistic rising interval.

Don't try to copy this particular emotional journey but do give each piece you write a clear sense of direction, with plenty of contrast.

♦ **Melodic shape and interest within each phrase**

There is a sense of growth within each phrase, and relaxation (each phrase ends below its highest point). Ascending and descending movement are carefully balanced, and there is variety of interval size (within fairly modest limits).

The melody makes reasonable use of the range of the oboe by spanning a range of a 12th. As shown on page 176, higher notes are possible – but it avoids the very lowest ones, which are difficult to produce.

♦ **Development of musical ideas**

The minor 7th in bar 3 is not left as an isolated event – there are other 7ths (including two major 7ths) in the added section, and the augmented octave in bar 10.

Bars 5^4–6^3 echo the rhythmic-melodic shape heard in bars 4^4–5^3. The 'echo' is not exact, of course, because the series doesn't allow it, and exact sequential repetition is foreign to the serial style. The five notes starting at *mf* in bar 8 are a more powerful version of the preceding five notes (starting at *mp* in bar 7).

♦ **Precise instructions for performance**

First, a *melody* instrument has been named. A melody instrument such as flute or oboe should be chosen for a serial melody, not a chordal instrument such as piano.

The music has a **tempo indication**, **dynamics** and **articulation marks** such as accents, tenuto signs and staccato dots. Frequent changes of dynamic and articulation are typical of serialism, because the music is often emotionally very intense, with every single note carefully chosen for its timbre and espressive effect.

Dynamics and articulation can help define phrases in the absence of traditional cadences, as well as serving to underline climaxes and other aspects of the music's emotional journey. But avoid peppering your work with symbols in the hope of impressing the examiner – whatever you write must have a clear musical purpose. And remember that while common Italian terms and abbreviations (such as **rit.**) are useful, it is often clearer to use plain English rather than obscure Italian terms.

Example 9.9 uses only the note names found in Example 9.1 and its magic square (on page 152). For instance, it always has G♯ and never A♭. However, in performance the player might find some 're-spelling' helpful. For example, the beginning of bar 4 might be clearer as B–D♯ (a straightforward major 3rd) rather than B–E♭ (a diminished 4th).

When you compose a melody, you are free to change the 'spelling' in this way if you are sure it is helpful, but don't use any such enharmonic equivalents in the given material when you copy it out.

Serial technique

In Example 9.9 there are three statements of the series after the given opening. The Edexcel AS exam requirement is for three or four added statements. You are free to write more, but there is no reward for doing so. Avoid using incomplete statements of the series, except possibly in a final passage.

After the given statement of P_0, Example 9.9 uses versions I_0, R_3 and P_8. This was purely a choice that worked well for this particular melody – it is not some standard set of versions that you must use. So how *do* you select the versions to use in your own work?

Variety is important. Use several different versions of the series:

✦ Include some I, R and/or RI versions …

✦ … and why not at least one transposed version (such as the R_3 in Example 9.9)?

✦ You *may* repeat P_0, perhaps at the end to give a feeling of recapitulation or completion. But this is not essential. And you don't have to end on the final note of P_0 – it's not a key note.

✦ If you do repeat P_0, invent a different rhythm for it.

✦ A version of the prime order other than P_0 may be useful at the end to provide a sense of recapitulation – for instance, Example 9.9 ended with P_8.

Remember that a new statement of the series must follow on well from the preceding music. When it begins it is usually best if we don't immediately hear again notes just heard, so as a general rule avoid using R straight after the same transposition of P (or RI after the same transposition of I). If R_0 had been used in bar 4 of Example 9.9, the notes F G♯ F♯ E would have followed the E F♯ G♯ F♮ of bar 3.

Activity 9.9

Play and study the following melody, which is again based on the series shown in Example 9.1.

(a) Identify the versions used after the opening P_0, and comment on their suitability.

(b) Using the magic square on page 152, identify any errors of serial technique such as missing accidentals, notes omitted, or completely wrong notes.

(c) Comment on any other omissions or weaknesses.

9.10 12-note serial melodies (ii)

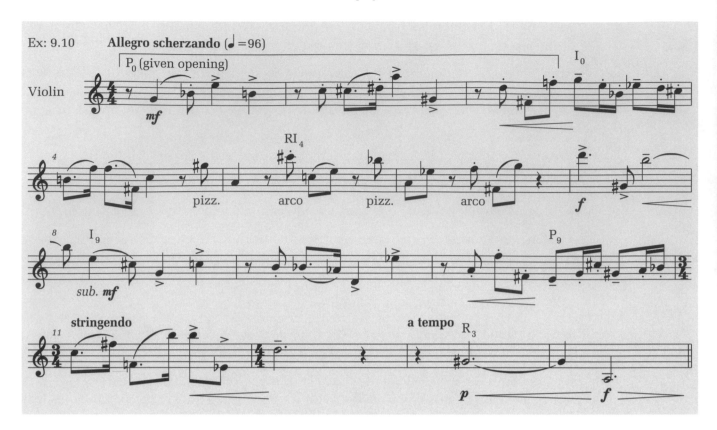

This example is more ambitious than Example 9.9. Try eventually to aim for something similar in your own work. The more ambitious nature of Example 9.10 is partly owing to:

✦ The **range** of the completed melody, which is two octaves and a 4th – slightly more than an octave wider than the range of the given opening. In your own work, at some point go higher and/or lower than the given opening. But avoid going to extremes where this might sound bizarre or might result in something unplayable.

✦ The **largest interval**, which is the augmented 12th (compound augmented 5th) at the end of bar 11 – considerably wider than the minor 9th in bar 2. In your own work, include some intervals which are at least as wide as the largest in the given opening, but very wide intervals should not be uncomfortably frequent, bizarre, or unplayable at your chosen tempo.

Structure

The given opening for Example 9.10 ends (rather unusually) with the start of a new phrase. This is to remind you that the beginnings and ends of musical phrases need not coincide with the beginnings and ends of statements of the series.

The last complete phrase (bars 10–12) is deliberately made longer than the rather similar phrase in bars 3–4, to give a little additional weight at this point. The $\frac{3}{4}$ bar (see the last bullet point in Section **9.11**) gives an added touch of rhythmic irregularity. The numerous rests help to create the light *scherzando* (playful) feel.

The overall structure is based on ternary form (but without an *exact* repeat of the opening section):

✦ Bars 1–4³ form section A

✦ Bars 4⁴–8¹ create a contrasting middle passage (B) which builds on bar 2 and has plenty of large intervals

✦ Bars 8²–12 are a kind of inversion of A, but not a literal repeat

✦ Bars 13–14 make a tiny coda.

Although 14 bars in length, Example 9.10 meets the exam requirement for a melody which is *about* 12 bars long. However, extend your answer beyond 12 bars only if there is a clear musical reason – here it is the provision of a two-bar coda. Avoid finishing before bar 12 since that is unlikely to give scope for a convincing answer.

Serial technique

Four complete statements of the series have been added to the given material, plus an additional incomplete statement (just two notes) at the end for the coda. This forms a useful rounding-off, with its inverted 'echo' of the two preceding notes and its reminder of intervals heard in bars 4 and 5.

The added versions of the series are:

✦ I_0, which is often successful after P_0 (as in Example 9.9). The opening shape of I_0 (G–E–B♭) neatly recalls the opening shape of P_0 (G–B♭–E).

✦ RI_4, which begins with notes not recently heard. Its opening C♯–C♮ (a descending augmented octave) echoes, although not exactly, the preceding major 7th, G♯–A.

✦ I_9 and P_9, which have the same subscript numeral and starting note (just as P_0 and I_0 did). This time, for variety, the I version precedes the P version. P_9 begins with E–G, again recalling the G–(B♭)–E outline at the start of P_0.

✦ Bars 13–14 contain the first two notes of R_3, which fit in well, not least because they are the same as the last two notes of I_0 – as used in bars 4^4–5^1 at the end of the first A section.

There are two **note repetitions**. We hear F twice in bar 4 and B twice in bar 11. The first note of each pair is a kind of anticipation, throwing weight onto the longer note which follows.

Activity 9.10

Describe the 'emotional journey' on which the listener is taken in Example 9.10.

9.11 Getting started on your own

Example 9.11.1 shows the prime order of a series on the top stave followed by a possible continuation (using I_0):

Ex: 9.11.1   Andante (♩. =54)
Cello
mp dolce
mf
rall.

P_0 spans an octave and a 4th, and includes two 7ths. In contrast, the largest interval in the continuation is a diminished 5th and the range is the minimum possible in a single statement of a series – a major 7th. Such restrictions seem disappointing, although of course much depends on what might happen in the rest of the melody. Now look at the rhythm of the continuation – particularly the way the phrase stops for an entire bar on its very first note, and the odd juxtaposition of semiquavers with notes twelve times as long at the end. Can you see why this is poor?

Here is the same opening with a continuation that uses I_0 in a different way:

This continuation has a more ambitious range, which equals that of the given opening, and the largest interval is a 7th – the same as the largest interval in P_0. In fact, it consists of a very literal inversion of the series, so that while P_0 has a typical arch-shaped profile, I_0 dips in the middle in a slightly odd way.

The interval of an octave should be avoided in serial writing because it over-emphasises the pitch class involved.

In the actual process of composition we can – and sometimes *should* – move notes to other octaves (**octave displacement**) in order to avoid the mechanical and obvious. For example, it might be more effective if the first note of I_0 (B) were an octave lower. Octave displacement can be used freely to turn small intervals into larger ones. For instance, the falling augmented 2nd (C♯–B♭) in bar 6 of Example 9.11.1 on the previous page has become a compound interval in bar 6 of the following:

This third continuation, which again uses I_0, is potentially the most successful. The range is greater, and the largest interval wider, and this time the second statement genuinely builds on the first. Large intervals are handled carefully, each being balanced by movement in the opposite direction. There is better rhythmic variety than in Example 9.11.2 (which was rhythmically rather dull), but none of the extreme contrasts in note lengths that prevented Example 9.11.1 from flowing well.

To be successful, a serial melody needs plenty of **controlled rhythmic variety**. Here are some tips about rhythm when you compose a serial melody:

✦ Don't repeat the whole rhythm of the given opening exactly, but …

✦ Do retain the general rhythmic style, and build on some important patterns

✦ Introduce one or two new rhythmic features without creating any unduly sudden or extreme contrasts

✦ Generally add more movement and activity as the piece progresses, while probably letting the music relax towards the end

✦ Use changes of time signature if, and only if, there is some good musical reason – for example, shorter bars sometimes give a greater sense of urgency (as in the $\frac{3}{4}$ bar with *stringendo* in Example 9.10).

Here are a couple of starter exercises that focus on the two main issues discussed in the preceding section: larger intervals and rhythm.

(a) The following phrase uses the minimum possible range for a complete series – a major 7th. By using octave displacements, rewrite it to include three or four large leaps at points that you consider to be musically effective. A large leap should be at least a minor 7th, but in this exercise avoid leaps larger than a 9th. You may change any or all of the given performance directions.

(b) Make *two* different arrangements of this series by adding musically interesting rhythms to the given pitches. One must be in $\frac{4}{4}$ time and the other in $\frac{3}{4}$. Choose a suitable instrument for each and add detailed performance directions.

9.12 12-note serial melodies: working method and exercises

Now we come to a method for completing a serial melody of about 12 bars. Here is an opening typical of the sort set in Edexcel AS Music papers:

Step 1   **Play and study the given opening**

Really get to know it. Remember that Example 9.12, like every given opening, has a unique combination of rhythms and pitches.

Step 2   **Decide on the character of the piece you will compose**

What kind of piece does the opening suggest? For example, does it seem dramatic, dance-like, humorous, lyrical, aggressive, gentle, melancholy … ?

Do the given performance directions match your ideas about the opening? Or should you opt – as you are allowed to – for a different tempo, dynamics and/or articulation? **But remember that you must not alter the pitches or rhythms of the given opening**.

Which instrument will you compose for? An opening is usually given on a treble stave but you are free to transpose it to a different octave and use a different clef if, for instance, you wish to write for bassoon or cello. Here, the low notes at the start don't suit the flute or oboe particularly well, although they are technically possible. But the given material would certainly sound good on either clarinet or violin.

Step 3   **Create a magic square for the series**

If you make a magic square by hand, the time is well spent. Remember that you constructed a magic square for this particular series in Activity 9.6 (b) on page 153.

Step 4   **Devise a possible outline structure**

It is important to realise that you can modify your initial outline as you work on the melodic detail later. For the moment, consider:

✦ On what kind of emotional journey will you take the listener? This will be directly related to the overall character of the music that you decided upon in Step 2.

✦ How will the melody be structured? For example, might it be based on a free interpretation of ternary form? Where will the points of climax and relaxation occur? How might the instrument's range and tone qualities be used in providing such contrasts?

✦ How many statements of the series might you add?

✦ Do you want musical phrases and statements of the series always to begin and end together?

✦ Testing ideas from the magic square, which version of the series might you begin with, and which versions might work well later?

Step 5   **Draft a melody**

Use all your ideas so far to produce an initial draft. As you compose, think carefully of how everything will sound in performance. Consider practicalities such as giving a wind player an opportunity to breathe, or a string player time to switch between *pizzicato* and *arco* – or, even more important, allowing time to attach or remove a mute. Add detailed performance directions as you go, while the sounds are fresh in your mind.

Step 6   **Review, revise, finalise**

✦ Thoroughly check your melody, making sure that you have copied the given material correctly, and that you have taken account of all the points above.

✦ Label the start of each version of the series you have used (I_3, R_0 and so on).

✦ Check that every note is present and correct, since it is easy to omit a note or write one in wrongly. In particular, check all necessary accidentals, especially naturals needed to cancel sharps or flats earlier in a bar. It may help if you number the notes from 1 to 12 in each version of the series you have used. Retrograde versions would, of course, start with the numbers 12, 11, 10 and so on.

✦ Make sure that your melody exploits the range and characteristics of the instrument you have chosen, but also check that it is playable. For instance, ensure that there are no notes out of range or any unnecessary difficulties such as wide leaps at a very fast speed. See page 176 for notes about writing for specific instruments.

Parts (a) and (b) of the next activity are short exercises designed to help you develop your melody-writing skills. The other three parts are questions of the length and type that you should expect in Edexcel AS Music exams.

In exam answers you must always start by **copying out the given material** and you must **label each use of the series** in your answer with the appropriate letter and subscript number. You are allowed to write a short commentary to explain how you have used the series, if you think it is helpful to the examiner.

(a) The following melody for clarinet at concert pitch consists of P₀ of a note row. Write out this opening and add to it **one** statement of I₅, maintaining the given melodic and rhythmic style. Include one or two intervals of a 9th in your answer and remember to add performance directions.

Now work the exercise again, this time adding a different version of the series, and a different rhythm from the one you used above.

(b) Add **two** statements (I₂ followed by R₅) to the opening below. Choose a suitable instrument and add performance directions. Let the music gradually expand in range and dynamic level up to the beginning of R₅, before again moving more narrowly and more quietly. Your largest interval should be a 9th.

In each of the following exercises, continue the given opening to make a complete serial melody of about 12 bars. Name the instrument you write for. You may alter any of the given performance instructions. Provide all necessary performance instructions in your added bars.

(c) Continue the opening printed as Example 9.12 on page 161. Remember that you constructed a magic square for this series in Activity 9.6 (b) on page 153.

9.13 Twelve-note music in two parts

The serialism exercise for Edexcel A2 Music is worked in examination conditions, although you are allowed access to an instrument if you wish. You are given the complete (P₀) statement of a series and have to complete a two-part piece lasting about 20 bars. Your added part may enter at any point during the given passage.

The challenge is to produce a contrapuntal piece with overall shape and coherence, good wide-ranging melodic lines in both parts, and sensible harmony. Serial harmony operates quite differently from tonal harmony, but requires equally careful control.

9.14 12-note music in two parts: harmony

In traditional two-part writing, such as that studied in Chapter 7, some intervals are used more frequently than others – 3rds, 6ths, 5ths and octaves are preferred, because these consonant intervals imply the chords vital for functional harmony.

In 12-note music all notes of the chromatic scale are equal and there is no functional harmony. It is therefore best to use all harmonic intervals fairly equally, except for octaves and unisons, as explained *opposite*. The choice of interval at each point in the music needs a lot of thought – you can't just write any two versions of the series at the same time and hope for the best. Always listen to the effect of what you write and ensure that it makes sense within the terms of the overall composition.

Here is a list of intervals with comments on their qualities. Intervals are mostly grouped in pairs, the second of each pair being the inversion of the first. In serial music the words consonance and dissonance aren't linked with traditional concepts of preparing and resolving discords, as they are in chorales and baroque counterpoint. We use them just in terms of sound quality. Dynamics can make a big difference – for example, a minor 2nd played very quietly is much less harsh than the same interval played loudly.

Major 3rd / minor 6th	consonant, sweet-sounding
Minor 3rd / major 6th	consonant, but less sweet than a major 3rd or minor 6th
Major 2nd / minor 7th	dissonant, fairly mild
Minor 2nd / major 7th	dissonant, harsh
Perfect 5th / perfect 4th	consonant, open and slightly bare
Dim. 5th / aug. 4th	dissonant, fairly mild but sometimes rather thin-sounding.

Compound intervals sound broadly similar to the corresponding simple intervals. For example, major 10ths and major 3rds are both consonant and sweet-sounding. But extremely wide compound intervals lose much of the character of the corresponding simple interval. For instance, intervals spanning two or three octaves plus a minor 2nd tend to sound much less dissonant than minor 2nds or minor 9ths.

Select a sound on an electric keyboard that sustains well, such as a flute or string voice, and try playing the notes A and B♭ together, first a semitone apart, and then separated by one, two and three octaves. Listen to the effect at different dynamic levels and note the difference between sustained dissonances and very brief ones. Experiment with other intervals in the same way.

12-note music usually has a fairly high level of dissonance, especially when composers are anxious to avoid any hint of tonality. It is uncharacteristic, and generally unwise, to write music with as many consonant intervals as those in Example 9.14.1 (i):

Examples on this and the following page are each printed on a single stave to make it easier to see the intervals involved. Two-part exercises are normally written on two separate staves.

Ex. 9.14.1

Ex. 9.14.2

Stave (ii) in this example is unusually dissonant, but consistently so, and is acceptable in the 12-note style. Stave (iii), adapted from (ii), has an odd mixture of dissonance and consonance and makes little musical sense.

Don't use octaves or unisons – they risk over-emphasising the pitch class involved. For the same reason, try to avoid the same pitch class appearing in succession in two different parts, as shown *left*.

Activity 9.14

Comment on the use of consonance and dissonance in the following passage.

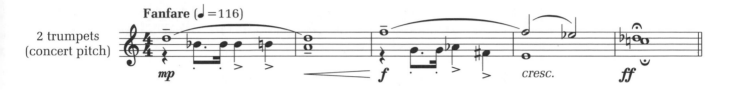

2 trumpets (concert pitch)

9.15 Using the series in two-part writing

There are two different ways in which you can use the series in two-part writing. They can both be used at different times within a single piece:

✦ **The simultaneous method**, in which one statement of the series appears in the top part and another one in the lower part

✦ **The divided method**, in which the notes of a single statement are divided between the two parts.

9.16 Using the series simultaneously in both parts

When deciding which versions to use simultaneously, aim for maximum variety of pitch and intervals. Be careful not to let the same pitch class appear simultaneously in both parts or in close succession.

If both parts begin at or about the same time it is better to use **two versions of the row that are of different types**, such as P_0 and I_6. If you combine versions of the *same* type, there is a risk that too many harmonic intervals will be identical. For instance, when P_7 is heard below P_0 there will be lots of perfect 4ths unless you manage to keep the parts well out of step with each other. Even so, as you can see in the following example, there are still seven perfect 4ths:

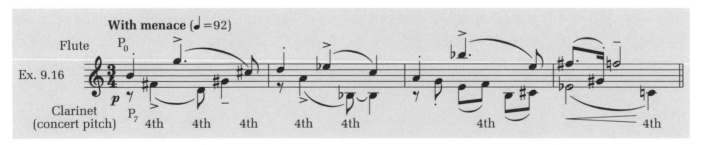

Ex. 9.16

Flute P_0

Clarinet (concert pitch) P_7 4th 4th 4th 4th 4th 4th 4th

Combining versions which don't begin with too many of the same pitch classes often works well. However, it is not effective to combine the same transposition of R and P, such as R_0 with P_0. While each has different pitch classes at the beginning, there is not enough variety in the middle of the two versions, for example:

| P_0: | B | G | C♯ | D | E♭ | C | A | B♭ | E | F♯ | G♯ | F |
| R_0: | F | G♯ | F♯ | E | B♭ | A | C | E♭ | D | C♯ | G | B |

Use the magic square to find what combinations will or won't work well. Refer to the one on page 152 as you read the following. We'll start rather negatively …

A **hexachord** is a set of six pitches.

R_7 is not a particularly good partner for P_0. The first six notes (**hexachord**) of each have no fewer than four notes in common. The second hexachords show a similar number of shared pitches. Can you find other versions of the series which overlap substantially with P_0?

I_9 makes a better partner for $P0$. Only two notes (G and C in our example) occur in the first hexachords of both versions. Better still, G comes at the beginning of P_0, but is note 6 in I_9. The two Cs are nearly as far apart. Find other suitable partners for P_0.

RI_4 in this particular series has a special property – its first hexachord has no notes in common with the first hexachord of P_0 and the second hexachords of each also have no common ground. This lack of overlap is called **hexachordal combinatoriality** – which we will abbreviate to 'HC'.

If P_0 and RI_4 are ideal partners in this series, so are P_1 and RI_5, P_2 and RI_6, P_3 and RI_7, and so on. Can you see why?

It is not always P_0 and RI_4 (and their related transpositions) which produce HC. For example, in Schoenberg's String Quartet No 4, the ideal partner for P_0 is I_5. So you will need to work out HC for any given series yourself, using a magic square.

Although the hexachords of P_0 and R_0 (and their related tranpositions) contain no overlapping pitches, these versions of the series don't combine well, for the reason shown at the foot of the previous page. In fact, you may not be able to find HC in some series, in which case look for the least repetitive pairings when using two versions of a series simultaneously.

Staggered starts

If instead of beginning at more or less the same time, one part begins considerably later than the other, things are surprisingly different:

✦ Two versions of the same type, such as two Ps or two Is, may now combine well since there will no longer be too many successive intervals of the same kind

✦ HC pairs will no longer be ideal partners because if one part enters while the other has reached its *second* hexachord, the two parts will share common pitches.

P_0 and R_0 may still not combine well – judge each case on its merits, and as always use the magic square to help you decide what will work effectively.

Activity 9.16

(a) If the first hexachord of P_0 is A G A♭ D E♭ F♯, what pitches will there be in the second hexachord?

(b) Create a magic square for the following series: F F♯ A G A♭ B♭ D C♯ E♭ E C B. Are there any HC possibilities?

9.17 Dividing the series between two parts

A series can be divided between two instruments, with the notes zigzagging between the parts, as shown in Example 9.17.1 on the next page. This gives each instrument an incomplete statement of the series, thus providing a new kind of melodic variety. Here the clarinet plays only notes 2, 3, 4, 7, 11 and 12 of the series, while the bassoon plays notes 1, 5, 6, 8, 9 and 10. There is no risk of octaves with this method.

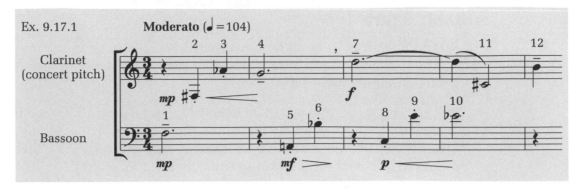

Ex. 9.17.1

Using the divided method is problematic at the start of an exam answer because you are given the series as a single line of melody, which you shouldn't split between the two parts. If you want to use the divided method as soon as you can, begin your addition near the *end* of the given melody. Then, as soon as the given part has ended, the instrument playing it can start sharing the remainder of your addition:

Ex. 9.17.2

After this, you can use the divided method without any further difficulty. Here are two further points on using the divided method:

Ex. 9.17.3

◆ You might occasionally want to let the two parts begin consecutive notes of the series at the same time (as a two-note chord). The example *left* shows the opening of the series quoted in Example 9.1 used in this way. It doesn't matter whether note 1 or note 2 appears in the top part.

◆ When dividing the series between parts it is a good idea to number the notes of the series and/or to write a short commentary to explain what you have done, so that the examiner doesn't overlook the subtlety of your methods!

Activity 9.17

(a) Divide the following series between oboe and bassoon parts, beginning as shown in (a) *below*: C C♯ D A♭ G F♯ E♭ A F B B♭ E.
Extend your piece by adding I_2 and dividing it between the parts.

(b) Stave (b) shows a new rhythmic arrangement of the series given *above*, for violin. Beginning very near the end, add a cello part, using the opening notes of any version of the series (other than I_2) that you consider fits well. Then divide the remaining notes of this version between the violin and cello.

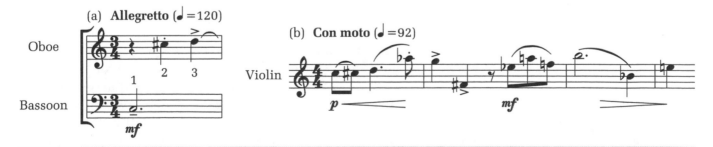

9.18 Structure

Before starting to compose a two-part serial piece, think carefully about the phrase structure and overall form. Remember, every piece should take the listener on some kind of emotional journey.

If you devise your own special musical form, be careful that it will make sense to the listener. If you use traditional forms such as ternary, avoid too much note-for-note repetition, as this is not characteristic of serial music and will reduce the number of bars in which you can demonstrate your creativity.

The return of the A section in ternary form can be abbreviated or varied. For example, you could keep some of the original rhythms while using different versions of the series from those in the opening A section. The following structure is another possibility:

+ A short opening section (A) which extends a little beyond the given opening and is rounded off with a clear ending.

+ Two, three or four brief sections (B, C, D), each contrasting with A but also connected with it in clearly audible ways. Motifs from A might be adapted and reused, for example. Each middle section could be complete in itself, with a double bar and complete break, or might be linked to the section following it.

+ A closing section, A^1 (meaning A varied) which refers more directly to the opening, but is not just a note-for-note repeat of all or most of A.

This succession of short sections may remind you of variations. However, there are few close parallels in serialism with the traditional variation techniques that you may have used in tonal compositions. Different serial composers have had different ideas of what variations are, and the distinction between variation form and the process of continuous variation essential to all serial writing is not always obvious.

9.19 Canon

Canon, widely used in the renaissance and baroque periods, is explained on page 68. Many serial composers have also used it to help give shape and direction to atonal writing. Canon is not an easy device and you don't *have* to use it, but you could, for example, employ it in one of the sections of a structure such as $ABCDA^1$, in the interests of variety.

In a serial canon we may hear two P versions of the series simultaneously (or two I, R or RI versions). Canon will work:

+ At the unison or octave. This may sound dull if the two parts enter in very close succession, and the repetition of one by the other is too obvious. Do you consider this to be the case with Example 9.19 (i) on the next page?

+ At the 2nd, 3rd, tritone, 6th or 7th – trial and error is needed to discover what will work well. Example 9.19 (ii) shows canon at the tritone.

+ Canon at the 4th or 5th – although in some circumstances this might be too suggestive of traditional tonic-and-dominant-style relationships.

A **canon by inversion**, as shown in Example 9.19 (iii), can be particularly effective. One part uses a P (or R) version of the series, while the other uses an I (or RI) version – the result is that all the intervals in the series are reflected back by the second part, rather like a mirror image, hence the name **mirror canon**. Webern uses this method throughout the first movement of his Quartet, Op 22. In a canon by inversion the tranpositions of the row don't have to be the same – for example, P_4 might be paired with I_{10}, if this works well in practice.

Ex. 9.19
(i)

A canon may begin with either the upper or lower part. You can choose how many beats separate the canonic part from the leading part. Example 9.19 *above* shows three possibilities. An entry after an uneven number of beats, as in (iii), can sometimes give the music a pleasing rhythmic irregularity.

When writing a canon, make sure that the distance between the parts results in strongly rhythmic contrasts when the parts are heard together, as in all three examples *above*.

Activity 9.19

(a) Write a canon at the octave for oboe and clarinet. The oboe, whose part is given, begins first. While the clarinet is completing the note row, the oboe should start any new version of the row which will fit with the end of the clarinet part.

(b) Write a canon by inversion for violin and cello. The violin enters first with P₀, as shown *below*. You must choose which version of I the cello should play.

9.20 Sample two-part piece

Here is a given opening – Example 9.20.2 *opposite* shows one possible completion.

Ex. 9.20.1

Character and scoring

The given opening is marked *Allegretto*, but a slower speed (Andante) has been chosen for the worked example. Dynamics and articulation have also been altered to provide a quieter, slightly mysterious beginning. As in the AS exam, you can change the given tempo marking and any other performance directions. Flute and bassoon have been chosen to play the piece, the characteristic timbres of the flute's lowest notes and the bassoon's highest range being deliberately exploited in the central section.

Structure

The structure is ABCDA^1 and the total length is 26 bars – which is acceptable, but a little more than you really need to write. We could have omitted one middle section or reduced the length of one or more sections.

The A section is connected to B by a tie from the final bassoon note. Sections B and D are quicker and lighter, with C providing a more lyrical and serious interlude. The beginning of section A^1 is marked by a return of the original tempo.

The emotional journey is underlined by the dynamics, which become progressively louder until we return suddenly to quiet music in A^1. The piece begins mysteriously, with rather fragmented lines, but there is more confidence in section B with its longer successions of quavers. In section C the bassoon (which had little to say in B) gains new eloquence, but the flute has relapsed, unable to summon much energy. Both instruments make a positive effort to interact and sound lively in section D, but the opening mood returns in A^1, which ends with two two-note sighing figures.

Handling of the series

The magic square indicates that I_9 works well (HC) with P_0. Section A twice combines these two versions – first with P_0 in the flute and I_9 in the bassoon, then the other way round from the end of bar 3. There is more than a straight swapping of parts – can you see what changes have been made?

Section B uses the divided method, with statements of P_0, I_6 and I_0 split between flute and bassoon. I_6 was chosen to follow P_0 because it starts with notes not recently heard – likewise, I_0 follows I_6 effectively. The repetition of P_0 here (and at the start of C) helps to link B with its surrounding sections and unify the composition – such repetition of the prime order is more useful in the middle of a relatively long two-part piece than in the middle of the much shorter serial melodies required in the AS exam.

Section C has a single statement of P_0 in the bassoon, while the flute plays R_{10}. The first and second hexachords start very similarly – a feature of this particular series. R_{10} was chosen partly to demonstrate retrograde movement, for additional variety. Its final note is B, but P_0 also ends on B. To avoid unisons or octaves, a small liberty has been taken – the final note of R_{10} has been transferred to the bassoon.

P_0 is avoided in Section D. Instead P_6 offers contrast – although also continuity since in this particular series the first hexachords of P_0 and P_6 contain the same notes in different orders. I_3 works well in the bassoon with P_6 (it has the same HC relationship as that between P_0 and I_9). Versions I_6 and P_3, another HC pair, are used in bars 19–21.

Section A^1 is largely a canon between P_0 and I_3. Can you see where the canon starts and ends? Where does the bassoon not follow the flute rhythm exactly? Why?

9.21 12-note two-part music: working method and exercises

The following method builds on the steps for completing a serial melody that we used for the AS exercises in Section **9.12** – you may like to re-read that section before continuing.

Step 1 **Play and study the given opening**

Every series is different, with its own characteristic intervals. You won't be able to apply a set method of handling the series to every exercise you do. In particular, don't try to memorise the succession and combination of versions in Example 9.20.2 on the previous page, and expect these to work every time.

Step 2 **Decide on the character of the piece you will compose**

You could choose two instruments that both have a treble range, such as two flutes. If so, the parts can cross – the second flute needn't always be below the first. But you may find it more interesting to write for instruments with different ranges, such as violin and cello.

Step 3 **Create a magic square for the series**

Work out which versions of the row are likely to work well together in combination and in succession, which will help create unity, and which will offer variety.

Step 4 **Devise a possible outline structure**

There is no particular number of statements that you must add to the given opening (as is the case at AS) – merely a requirement that the complete piece should be about 20 bars in length.

Step 5 **Draft the two parts**

Try to give each part a wide compass that exploits the timbres and characteristics of the instrument concerned, and that includes some large leaps, but also check that the parts are playable, with no notes out of range or unnecessary technical difficulties. See page 176 for some notes about writing for specific instruments.

Aim for effective harmony – avoid octaves and unisons, and the same pitch class appearing in succession in two different parts. Remember that you shouldn't include too many consonant intervals in succession since that could make the music sound unintentionally tonal. Above all, don't mix areas of harsh dissonance and areas of sweet consonance in a random manner.

Look for opportunities to display your understanding of serial techniques, such as the occasional use of R or RI versions of the row, and perhaps a short canonic section.

Step 6 **Review, revise, finalise**

Make sure that you have included the given material correctly and that there are no errors or omissions in your use of the series. In particular, check that all necessary accidentals are present – especially naturals needed to cancel sharps or flats earlier in a bar.

Each version of the series used must be labelled (I_3, R_0 and so on) and you may find it helpful to number the notes from 1 to 12 in each version of the series you have used. Retrograde versions should start with the numbers 12, 11, 10 and so on. You can, as in the AS exam, include a brief written commentary to explain your methods, if you feel this will assist in making your intentions clear to the examiner.

Compose two-part pieces based on the openings given below. Each should last for about 20 bars, including the given opening. Choose the instruments, indicate what they are, and remember to label each version of the row that you use. You may alter any or all of the given performance instructions. Provide all necessary instructions in your added bars.

In conclusion

12-note serialism is a big topic and this chapter has not aimed to cover everything. For example, there has been no word about some of the more learned devices such as rotation. The intention has been to help you develop enough ordinary techniques to write some genuine *music*, and to realise that serialism, however strange, requires as much skill and judgement as any other type of music.

Reference section

Other major and minor keys

The tables of keys and scales on pages 8 and 12 include key signatures of up to four sharps and four flats – the ones most likely to be encountered in techniques exams. However, you should be prepared to work in other keys since a test may modulate to a more remote key.

The table *below* illustrates major and minor keys that were not covered earlier. The first column shows the scale with accidentals before each note that needs them, the second shows the scale with its key signature, and the third shows you how the key signature is written in the bass clef.

B major

G# minor (relative minor of B major)

F# major

D# minor (relative minor of F# major)

D♭ major

B♭ minor (relative minor of D♭ major)

G♭ major

E♭ minor (relative minor of G♭ major)

The symbol **x** before note 7 in the scales of G♯ minor and D♯ minor indicates a double sharp. F**x** is *two* semitones above F – in other words, the same pitch as G – while C**x** is *two* semitones above C – the same pitch as D.

In the case of minor keys, only the harmonic minor scale is included in the table *opposite*. If you need a melodic minor scale, remember that:

+ The ascending melodic minor scale differs from the harmonic in having a raised note 6.

+ The descending melodic minor differs from the harmonic minor in having a lowered note 7. It needs an accidental only when one is necessary to cancel the effect of a raised 7 earlier in the same bar. For instance, in D minor you would have to write C♮ for the lowered seventh if C♯ had occurred earlier in the bar.

The scales of F♯ major and G♭ major are **enharmonic equivalents**, which means that they sound the same but are notated differently. The scales of D♯ minor and E♭ minor are also enharmonic equivalents.

Which you choose depends on context. In the key of E major, the dominant is B major, and if you needed to modulate to the dominant key of B major, it would be sensible to choose F♯ major because it merely means adding two sharps to the four already present in E major. But in the key of A♭ major, if you wanted to modulate to the dominant of the dominant key, it would make more sense to choose G♭ major rather than F♯ major, again because it would involve far fewer accidentals.

Using score-writing software

In some exams you are allowed to submit your work in the form of printout from computer score-writing software. Your teacher will know whether or not this is possible in your paper. If it is, and you decide to use a score-writing package, make sure that you really know how to operate it. Such software does not necessarily produce clear and correct notation without some user intervention, and it is not always easy to use – take advice from someone who has plenty of experience with the package you are working with. In particular avoid:

+ Cramped or over-generous spacing between staves or within individual bars

+ Incorrect beaming of short notes and faulty grouping of rests

+ Unnecessarily-repeated accidentals

+ Wrong bar-numbering where the music begins with an upbeat (the first *complete* bar should be bar 1)

+ Labelling parts wrongly (for example, chorales are not for piano)

+ Expecting the package to know what you mean without your telling it precisely (most computers still can't think!).

Remember that you will probably have to input the given material as well as your own added sections, and that this may take a surprisingly long time. You will be expected to include all aspects of the given material, including any figured bass or chord symbols, although you may be allowed to add such indications in neat handwriting if you cannot do it using the software.

You must also make sure that the given material is transcribed completely correctly and doesn't include, for instance, subtle alterations to the rhythm, different beaming or inappropriate accidentals, such as using A♯ where B♭ is required.

Whatever you decide to do, it is still good to learn how to write music accurately, neatly and quickly!

Ranges of instruments

In tests for which you can choose a suitable melody instrument you need to keep in mind the available range. Sensible working ranges for some of the more common instruments that might be used in baroque counterpoint or serialism tests are listed *below*. Good players can manage higher notes, but you should not normally expect to take a part in baroque style beyond the range shown by notes in black type.

Parts for transposing instruments, such as the clarinet in B♭, are normally written at 'concert pitch' (as they are intended to sound) in techniques tests, so the ranges *below* show the actual limits you should use.

Recorder

In baroque music, the term recorder refers to the treble recorder – notice that it cannot play lower than F above middle C.

Flute

Be careful not to overuse the lower notes, which tend to be rather quiet. The flute's brightest range extends upwards from D, a 9th above middle C.

Oboe

Avoid rapid passages in the lower part of the register and remember that it is difficult to play quietly on the very lowest notes.

Clarinet in B♭

In techniques tests, clarinet parts are usually expected to be written at sounding ('concert') pitch rather than being transposed.

Alto saxophone

The part should normally be written at sounding pitch in techniques tests. Use the lowest notes sparingly. The tenor sax sounds a perfect 5th lower than the alto.

Bassoon

Like the oboe, the lowest notes of the bassoon's range should be used sparingly. The tenor clef (see *below*) is sometimes used in the highest register.

Trumpet in B♭

Trumpet parts are usually expected to be written at sounding pitch in techniques tests, rather than being transposed. Use the lowest notes sparingly.

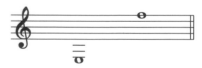

Violin

In baroque styles it is best to avoid taking violin parts too low as they may sound dull and may bring the melody uncomfortably close to the bass.

Cello

Like the bassoon, the tenor clef (𝄢), which indicates the position of middle C, is sometimes used for parts that make extensive use of the highest register.